Assignments • Stock • Prints

www.golfcoursephotography.com
001805.962.8466

Top 100
Golf Courses
of Britain & Ireland

2007 - 2008

Swinley Forest Golf Club - Photograph by Andy Taylor

Top 100
Golf Courses
of Britain & Ireland

2007 - 2008

Wentworth Club - East Course

KEITH BAXTER

Top 100
Golf Courses
of Britain & Ireland
2007 – 2008

Keith Baxter

June 2007

Graphic design by Nick Oliver.
Course descriptions by Keith Baxter, Jim McCann and Andy Newmarch.
Photography by Top 100 Golf Courses except where stated.

ISBN 978-0-9554956-0-1

Published by Top 100 Golf Courses Limited
Stone Farm, Bere Ferrers, Devon, PL20 7JY
www.top100golfcourses.co.uk

Printed in Hong Kong

Uncaptioned photographs
Front cover — Rosapenna (Sandy Hills) Aidan Bradley, back cover — Kingsbarns

Contents

The Top 100 Golf Courses of Britain & Ireland

18th Green St Andrews Old Course

Acknowledgements

The views in this book are the combined and rounded opinions of dozens of club professionals, golf course architects, club officials and thousands of passionate golfers. We are genuinely grateful that so many people visit the Top 100 website (www.top100golfcourses. co.uk) every day and are especially indebted to those who take the time to post passionate course reviews, hundreds of which are included in this book.

The quality of the photographs we receive via email every day is quite stunning and we are grateful to those who have allowed us to print their remarkable images. This book would not have been possible without their input.

Thanks must also go to the many golf club officials, too numerous to mention by name. We are touched by their kind words, generous support and for allowing us to play and photograph their stunning golf courses.

We also acknowledge the golf magazines and their teams of panellists who take the business of ranking golf courses as seriously as we do.

It's impossible for us to name everyone who has helped us, but we would especially like to mention: Stewart Abramson, Aidan Bradley, Paul Edwards, Cédric Hannedouche, Jim McCann, Kevin Murray, Alex Sherratt, Andy Taylor and Rod Wiltshire.

Special thanks go to our close friends and family, whose patience has been well and truly tried.

Ballybunion (Old) 18th

The Top 100 Ranking, Rating and Review Systems

Rankings

1st to 100th or in some cases 125th or more

First of all, we acknowledge that many golf magazines do a great biennial job of ranking our greatest British & Irish golf courses and long may they continue to do so. However, our process is unique and many have told us that we actually do it better than the magazines themselves.

With input from a statistician at Cambridge University, we built a comprehensive database that contains historical ranking information from golf magazines and other publications. Then we applied a series of rules and weightings favouring the world rankings, the most recent rankings and the frequency that courses appear on ranking lists. This process has, in effect, created our unique ranking for each course and it is perhaps best described as the consensus of consensuses.

Naturally, ranking golf courses is not an objective process in the first place, but we feel that nobody does it better. And, to add our own dimension, we factor in our own Top 100 ranking, generated by course review ratings posted on the Top 100 website (www.top100golfcourses.co.uk) by passionate golfers from all walks of life.

ALBATROSS - Excellent	●●●●●
EAGLE - Very Good	●●●●●
BIRDIE - Good	●●●●
PAR - Average	●●●
BOGEY - Poor	●●
DOUBLE BOGEY - Very Poor	●

Ratings
The main part of the Top 100 website course review process requires the course reviewer to rate the course for which they are writing a review. We decided to make the rating system simple and set no specific rules for rating a golf course except, naturally, that the reviewer should have played it. Important factors, such as course design, condition, difficulty, variety and historical importance are all left for the reviewer to judge.

Each course can only receive one rating for each posted review. Rather than using a star rating system, we decided to use a golf ball rating. If, for example, reviewer a) decides to give Carnoustie a four-ball rating and reviewer b) gives Carnoustie a six-ball rating, then Carnoustie will show five balls. However, if reviewer a) gives Carnoustie a five-ball rating and reviewer b) gives Carnoustie six balls, then Carnoustie will show five and a half balls. The Top 100 website automatically calculates the number of golf balls allocated to each course by averaging the reviewers' ratings and then we have a rounding up process implemented to the nearest half or full ball.

We took a snapshot of the website's reviewers' golf ball ratings for each course in December 2006 and the golf ball rating is shown on each course page in this book but you'll need to see the website for the absolute latest position.

Once again we have created our own Top 100 list based on the golf ball rating system (see page 218). If fact, we decided to print the Top 200 and we've factored these statistics into our comprehensive ranking database.

Reviewers' Comments
All the comments on the left hand pages (even numbers) are edited extracts from reviews posted on the Top 100 website by passionate golfers. Anybody can write a course review and, since we published our first book in June 2005, more than 2,000 new course reviews have been written and posted online by all types of golfer from the professional to the high handicapper. We think these honest comments really cut to the chase and bring this book and the Top 100 website to life.

If you want to influence the Top 100 rankings and have something to say about the Top 100 courses you've played, then visit the website at www.top100golfcourses.co.uk and write a course review. If you agree or disagree with any of the course reviews posted online then you have the right to reply via our new online reply facility. We look forward to serving you online.

The Top 100 Team

Prestwick Golf Club

AIDAN BRADLEY

Golf Course Photographer

Where To Find Them

Pos	Course	Move	Pos	Course	Move
1	Royal County Down	Up 2	61	Royal Cinque Ports	Up 3
2	St Andrews (Old)	Down 1	62	Blairgowrie (Rosemount)	Down 9
3	Turnberry (Ailsa)	Up 3	63	Carton House (Montgomerie)	New
4	Muirfield	Down 2	64	County Louth	Down 32
5	Royal Portrush (Dunluce)	No move	65	Pennard	Down 13
6	Kingsbarns	Up 10	66	Rye (Old)	No move
7	Royal Birkdale	Down 3	67	Worplesdon	Up 18
8	Carnoustie (Championship)	No move	68	Enniscrone	Up 19
9	Woodhall Spa (Hotchkin)	Up 9	69	Aberdovey	Down 31
10	Ballybunion (Old)	Down 3	70	Woburn (Duke's)	Up 8
11	Royal Dornoch (Championship)	Up 9	71	West Sussex	Up 1
12	Lahinch (Old)	Down 2	72	Machrie	Up 3
13	Loch Lomond	No move	73	Hunstanton	Down 15
14	Waterville	Down 5	74	Belfry (Brabazon)	Up 24
15	Portmarnock (Old)	Down 5	75	Alwoodley	Down 5
16	Royal Liverpool	Up 1	76	Hankley Common	New
17	Royal St George's	Down 8	77	Bearwood Lakes	New
18	European Club	Up 4	78	Woburn (Marquess)	New
19	Sunningdale (Old)	Down 7	79	Grove	New
20	Royal Lytham & St Annes	Up 9	80	Adare	Up 4
21	Ganton	No move	81	Moortown	Up 8
22	Wentworth (West)	Up 2	82	Chart Hills	New
23	Walton Heath (Old)	Up 2	83	Aldeburgh	New
24	Royal Troon (Old)	Down 7	84	Berkshire (Blue)	Down 30
25	Cruden Bay	Up 18	85	West Hill	Up 9
26	Royal Porthcawl	Down 3	86	Burnham & Berrow	Down 18
27	Gleneagles (King's)	Up 1	87	Woburn (Duchess)	Down 1
28	Prestwick	Up 7	88	Addington	New
29	Machrihanish	Up 16	89	Murcar	New
30	Nairn	Down 3	90	Castlerock	New
31	St George's Hill	Up 17	91	St Andrews Bay (Torrance)	New
32	North Berwick	Up 9	92	Trevose (Championship)	Down 9
33	Royal Aberdeen	Up 9	93	Castletown	Down 5
34	Saunton (East)	Down 4	94	Walton Heath (New)	New
35	St Enodoc (Church)	Up 25	95	Royal North Devon	New
36	Carne	Up 46	96	Portstewart (Strand)	Down 1
37	Hillside	Down 6	97	St Andrews (New)	Down 50
38	Old Head	Down 1	98	Lindrick	Down 8
39	Western Gailes	Down 3	99	Royal Ashdown Forest (Old)	No move
40	Silloth-on-Solway	Up 9	100	Saunton (West)	Down 29
41	Doonbeg	Up 26			
42	Formby	Down 8			
43	Swinley Forest	Down 14			

Table shows current book ranking 2007 (GB&I) v 2005 (British Isles).

Pos	Course	Move	Course	
44	Royal West Norfolk	Up 19	Ashburnham	46
45	Sunningdale (New)	Down 22	Pyle & Kenfig	55
46	K Club (Palmer)	Down 7	Killarney (Killeen)	59
47	Tralee	Up 27	Tenby	69
48	Mount Juliet	Down 4	St Pierre	73
49	Gullane (No.1)	Up 12	Wisley (Garden & Mill)	76
50	County Sligo (Championship)	Up 6	Southerness	77
51	Druids Glen	Up 6	Southport & Ainsdale	80
52	Gleneagles (Queen's)	Down 2	Celtic Manor (Wentwood Hills)	81
53	Island	New	Little Aston	91
54	Royal St David's	Down 28	Ferndown	92
55	Wentworth (East)	Up 7	Woking	93
56	Notts	Down 5	Liphook	96
57	Ballyliffin (Glashedy)	Up 22	Downfield	97
58	Berkshire (Red)	Down 18	Skibo Castle	100
59	Nefyn (Old)	Up 6		
60	Rosapenna (Sandy Hills)	New		

Above courses relegated from the Top 100

Royal County Down

ROYAL COUNTY DOWN GOLF CLUB
Newcastle, County Down, BT33 0AN, Northern Ireland
Telephone: +44 (0) 28 4372 3314
Website: www.royalcountydown.org
Architect: Old Tom Morris, Harry Vardon
Visitors: Contact in advance – not Sat or Wed

Average Reviewers' Score:

Reviewers' Comments

This is the best course in Ireland… The benchmark for all other courses… Best course I've ever played or maybe ever likely to… Work of art disguised as a golf course… Unimaginably good design… Many elevation changes to make this a literal rollercoaster of a golfing ride… Your knees shake on every drive you have to thread between tufty bunkers and thick rough… There's an eerie atmosphere here, almost scary, like you have gone back in time… Double bogeys lurk on every hole… Every hole is visually a treat… Only weakness is a few average holes toward the finish… Course would play better if the nines were reversed… A special, special place… It was special, as it inspired me to spend over £100 in the shop after the round… The welcome we got from the local pro was so warm and friendly it just added to our great day… Newly extended clubhouse is very impressive… No matter the length of your stay, this course must be at the head of the list… A truly great course.

Royal County Down is at Newcastle, a little holiday town nestling at the feet of the majestic Mountains of Mourne. It's an exhilarating location for a classic links golf course where the Bay of Dundrum sweeps out into the Irish Sea and where the mighty peak of Slieve Donard (3,000 ft.) casts its shadow over the town.

Old Tom Morris was paid the modest sum of four guineas to design the course and it opened for play in 1889. Harry Vardon modified it in 1908, the same year King Edward VII bestowed royal patronage on the club. Old Tom was presented with an idyllic piece of ground on which to design a golf course. The sand dunes are rugged but beautifully clad in purple heather and yellow gorse, the fairways are naturally undulating, shaped by the hands of time.

Measuring more than 7,000 yards from the back tees, it's a brute. Factor in the ever-changing wind and you have as stern a test as any Open Championship venue.

The course has a level of eccentricity, a number of blind drives and some bunkers are fringed with coarse grass, which gathers the ball with alarming regularity, but this simply adds to the charm. If a measure of a great golf course is the number of holes you can remember, then Royal County Down is one of the greatest courses of them all.

Kevan Whitson – Professional writes: The championship links at Newcastle, once found and played, will never be forgotten. It's as tough as they come and yet a delightful walk under the shadow of the ever changing Mourne Mountains.

The links are comprised of two loops weaving their way through magnificent dunes and wild gorse bushes with each tee inviting a sharp intake of breath at what lies before you, from the demanding tee shots to the superb greens protected by bunkers in their most natural state. The greens are subtle and very fast and feature run off areas to frustrate the very best who play this wonderful game. Stay in the fairways, play to the front of the greens and this great links will allow you safe passage and a day to remember.

Steve Ward

St Andrews (Old)

ST ANDREWS LINKS
St Andrews, Fife, KY16 9SF, Scotland
Telephone: +44 (0) 1334 466666
Website: www.standrews.org.uk
Architect: Unknown
Visitors: Book well in advance - by ballot

Average Reviewers' Score:

Reviewers' Comments
A dream-like place and a must-play for any true golfer... Played the auld lady over 100 times and it's still an amazing experience... Memories I will have for the rest of my life... Found the course a slight let-down and, dare I say, somewhat bland in parts... Spine tingling the whole way around... An incredible experience to play the most historic course in the world... Enjoyed every single minute... It really is like nothing else you have played or will play... The most natural, unique, fair and fun course I've ever played... The buzz around the 1st tee, the anticipation, the trepidation... I get goosebumps every time I walk up the 18th... I love this course, I love the town of St Andrews, and I love the people of the town... Everyone should play the Old Course at least once, but everyone should spend a week every year in the village itself... Pay your money and soak up the history and the ambience for all it's worth... You must make the pilgrimage.

Every true golfer should play this course at least once. It sends shivers down the spine when the starter announces your name, setting those first tee nerves jangling. Oozing familiarity with names like the Swilcan burn (and bridge), Valley of Sin, Hell bunker, the Road hole, the Principal's Nose and Elysian fields.

The Old Course greens are the most extraordinary and interesting putting surfaces in the world. There is little definition between where the fairway, fringe and green stops or starts and the fairways are probably faster and certainly more undulating than the average golf club's greens. And their size is absolutely staggering – they are gigantic, occupying more than an acre in some cases.

So, get yourself in the ballot and keep your fingers crossed. You will definitely remember the Old course experience for the rest of your life.

Quotes courtesy of St Andrews Links:
Paul Casey: "The hairs on the back of my neck still stand up, especially when I stand on the 1st and 18th tees."
Tom Doak: "Some people love St Andrews as a monument. I love it as a golf course."
Bobby Jones: "The more I studied the Old Course, the more I loved it; and the more I loved it, the more I studied it."
Jack Nicklaus: "The Old Course at St Andrews will always hold a special place in my heart. I fell in love with it the first time I played it in 1964, and in my five decades of travelling the globe, playing and creating golf courses, I have experienced no place like St Andrews. It has a certain mystique and a unique charm that is timeless."
Gene Sarazen: "I wish that every man who plays golf could play St Andrews once."
Tiger Woods: "Without a doubt, I like it best of all the Open venues. It's my favourite course in the world."

Kevin Murray

THE WESTIN TURNBERRY RESORT
Turnberry, Ayrshire, KA26 9LT, Scotland
Telephone: +44 (0) 1655 334032
Website: www.turnberry.co.uk
Architect: Philip Mackenzie Ross
Visitors: Contact Golf Reservations Office

Average Reviewers' Score:

Reviewers' Comments

Ailsa is the best place to play golf in the entire world… It literally took my breath away… Epitomises what I expected links golf to be on my first trip to GB… This may be the one links course I would choose to play if limited to only one for the rest of my life… Loved it, even though my golf game had deserted me that day… Some majestic holes both by the coast and inland… Drive off the championship tee on 9 is the highlight… Would be great if they could take a couple of the coastal holes from the Kintyre course to make those magic holes around the turn last a bit longer… Seaside holes are unmatched among the great championship courses and is a wonderful test with no weak holes… A complete course, and I loved every minute of it… Tranquil setting on a summer's day is simply heaven on earth… A must play for anyone who is interested in golf… Can't wait to go back again… Nothing else to say except Wow!

Anthony Münder

The Ailsa course at Turnberry is probably the most scenic Open Championship course – often referred to as Scotland's Pebble Beach – and possibly contains the finest stretch of coastal holes in Britain. Located right next to the Irish Sea, with craggy rocks and superb views across to the Isles of Mull and Arran, it's an unusual links course, because there are no dunes protecting the holes that run close to the sea (4th to the 11th). This makes for an interesting challenge when there's a freshening wind.

Essentially it's an out and back layout with the prevailing wind usually at your back for the outward nine. The stretch of holes from the 4th to the 11th is thrilling and the scenery breathtaking. The tee shot on the par four 9th fills you with trepidation as you drive over the rugged shoreline to a blind fairway. This signature hole, called "Bruce's Castle" takes you past the famous lighthouse and Robert the Bruce's ruined castle.

Paul Burley – Director of Golf writes:
Long regarded as one of the finest courses in the world, the Ailsa course at Turnberry came to international prominence with the famous duel between Jack Nicklaus and Tom Watson over the four days of the 1977 Open. Tom Watson won in 1977, Greg Norman in 1986 and Nick Price in 1994... all testimony to Turnberry's greatness. The Ailsa will once again host The Open Championship in 2009.

The scenic glories of the Ailsa Course are to be savoured – the granite dome of Ailsa Craig, the low form of the tip of Argyll and the peaks of Arran highlighting the changing patterns of light and shade. Closer at hand, the lighthouse, and the ninth's lovely back tee are other symbols of Turnberry, the hole's title, Bruce's Castle adding an historic echo.

The course itself is a wonderful test of links golf, difficult but very fair. Reasonably generous fairways provide few awkward stances, but the weather often changes by the hour to augment the challenge of this superb course.

THE HONOURABLE COMPANY OF EDINBURGH GOLFERS *Average Reviewers' Score:*
Duncur Road, Gullane, East Lothian, EH31 2EG, Scotland
Telephone: +44 (0) 1620 842123
Website: www.muirfield.org.uk
Architect: Old Tom Morris, Harry Colt and Tom Simpson
Visitors: Welcome Tue/Thu – book in advance

Reviewers' Comments

It's a privilege to walk in the Muirfield gate… Best course in Scotland… Muirfield is pure golf – an intellectual, cerebral experience rather than a sensual one… Cannot understand the high ranking. There was nothing memorable about the course… I've played here twice and they are some of my memorable moments in my entire golfing career… The course was good but not great… Probably the most perfectly laid out course in the world… Is as fair as a golf course can be… Course puts pressure on your game on every shot – from the driver to the short game… Bunkers are absolutely brutal… Green complexes are among the best… Every shot is a challenge, every hole difficult and demanding… You finish a round here mentally drained… Visitors think that this "stuffy" atmosphere is unwelcoming but this has probably been the norm since 1744… You want stuffy, try playing Augusta National… The club itself is very gracious, as long as you have made the proper arrangements.

Jim McCann

Muirfield is the course of The Honourable Company of Edinburgh Golfers whose records date back to 1744 when the club drafted the original 13 rules of golf in readiness for their inaugural competition played for the Silver Club.

Host to 15 Opens, most recently in 2002, Muirfield is considered by many of the top professionals to be one of the fairest Open Championship golf courses and is blessed with a collection of superb golf holes. Fairways have that lovely crisp seaside turf, there's some unbelievable bunkering and there's thick, thick rough to contend with. The greens are relatively small too, making you think carefully about your approach shots.

Courtesy of The Honourable Company of Edinburgh Golfers – Donald Steel writes:

Ask a dozen golfers to classify courses and you will get as many different answers but over Muirfield there is absolute unanimity. Some confer upon it the accolade of perfection although such eminence is as difficult to define as the perfect round of golf. It would be asking a lot for a course to combine the natural simplicity of Westward Ho!, the severity of Carnoustie, the strategic cunning of St Andrews and the scenic splendour of Turnberry. Even then, personal taste can be the deciding factor but one thing over which few will argue is that Muirfield embraces more of the qualities that a perfectionist seeks in his ideal course.

Architecturally, it is a gem. A clockwise outward half encases an anticlockwise inward nine, an arrangement that ensures that players have to make incessant adjustment for wind direction. To whom goes the credit for such design has never been freely acknowledged. As with so many of our great links, it is an amalgam of several minds but it is the variety and fairness of Muirfield's demands that have won it universal fame.

As a choice for championships, international matches or Club outings, it is a constant favourite. There is no other that has hosted the Open, the Amateur, the Ryder, Walker and Curtis Cups, the British Mid Amateur, the Vagliano Trophy, the University Match and a host of other regional tournaments. Apart from the classic challenge it presents, the delights of its surroundings are attractively congenial. Muirfield is second to none.

Jim McCann

Royal Portrush (Dunluce)

ROYAL PORTRUSH GOLF CLUB
Dunluce Road, Co. Antrim, BT56 8JQ, Northern Ireland
Telephone: +44 (0) 28 7082 2311
Website: www.royalportrushgolfclub.com
Architect: Harry Colt
Visitors: Contact in advance - Restrictions Wed & Fri pm, Sat & Sun am

Average Reviewers' Score:

Reviewers' Comments

Dunluce is probably the fairest world-class links that I have played... Hats off to Harry Colt for a design that will surpass many expectations... Each time I play I find something new that I like... Lots of variety with left and right hand dogleg holes... First nine is definitely the harder nine with tighter driving holes... First 15 holes are the best 15 that I have played... Good layout but lacked something I can't quite put my finger on... Classic links which I would play anytime I had the opportunity... Undulating land is just marvellous for golf... Setting is absolutely breathtaking... Few bunkers as they are not needed... Hardly a blind shot to play... Pity the last two holes are a little bland... This is Colt's best links and a challenge from 1st tee to 18th green... No poor holes, just pleasure all the way... Worthy of its high rating... Wonderful golf course which lived up to my expectations (and they were high!)... Play the Valley Course as well.

Surely Royal Portrush has the most dramatic entrance to any golf course. As you wind your way towards the course along the coastal road, the crumpled, undulating links land suddenly appears in front of you, flags fluttering in the breeze. This is a seaside links paradise, located in an evocative setting on the north Antrim coastline, blessed with magnificent ocean views. On a clear day (from the 3rd tee) you can see the Paps of Jura and the island of Islay.

Fairways nestle in natural valleys between towering sand dunes. The small greens blend perfectly into the landscape. Greens are generally protected by natural grassy hummocks rather than sand bunkers. The most spectacular parts of the course are down by the shore with elevated tees and greens perched on the very edge of the course above the seashore.

Gary McNeill – Head Professional writes:
Royal Portrush Golf Club can only be described as a marvellous creation, the work of a genius, set on the most spectacular coastline.

The course begins on the outskirts of Portrush town and by the time you've climbed gently from the 2nd green to the 3rd tee, the true splendour of what lies ahead is revealed. Virtually all holes can be seen from here, together with stunning scenery – the hills of Donegal to the west and the island of Islay off the west coast of Scotland to the east.

As you journey on, you reach the 5th green – perched high up above White Rocks beach – with spectacular views along the coastline, past the ruins of Dunluce Castle and on to the Giant's Causeway. Continuing on through the turn, you twist your way through the dunes, each hole taking your breath away, the magnificence of Harry Colt's creation unfolding in front of you. Reaching the 14th tee, you face the prospect of a 200-yard carry over a deep ravine to a green perched up above you. No wonder it's named "Calamity"!

The downhill 15th – "Purgatory" – begins the run home toward the town once again, past the famous "Big Nellie" bunker on the 17th to the demanding 469-yard finishing hole… hopefully negotiating eleven bunkers along the way. It's the most demanding finish to a course which can only be described as exhilarating and fair with no blind shots.

Kevin Murray

Kingsbarns

KINGSBARNS GOLF LINKS
Kingsbarns, St Andrews, Fife, KY16 8QD, Scotland
Telephone: +44 (0) 1334 460860
Website: www.kingsbarns.com
Architect: Kyle Phillips
Visitors: Course closed Dec–Mar – contact in advance

Average Reviewers' Score:

Reviewers' Comments

Maybe a little bit controversial for the traditionalists but in my opinion this is the best golf course in Scotland, bar none… This course has it all, a mix of holes that keep you thoroughly entertained… Magical place to play golf… It's expensive but make it an expensive treat and you won't be disappointed… It's worth every penny… My socks were well and truly blown off… There is something here for golfers of all levels… Kingsbarns really stretches your golf brain… Design has not taken the mere mortal into account… Standing on the first tee I felt like I was playing an historic Open rota course, it just had that X-factor for me… Inspired variety of holes, hugely memorable, the sea in sight all the time… True test of golf, especially if the wind blows… Course feels so natural… Numerous standout holes and yes, the 12th is as good as everybody says… At least two of the best holes I have ever played… Pay the money and enjoy… In short, believe the hype.

Kevin Murray

American architect Kyle Phillips studied various courses, including Royal Dornoch, to ensure that the end design would look natural. The earthmovers then rumbled in and shifted hundreds of thousands of tonnes of earth to create the moonscape that is now Kingsbarns. The course opened in July 2000 to rapturous applause.

One of the many delights of Kingsbarns is that you can see the North Sea from virtually every part of the course. What's more, it has its own burn (the Cambo), which was uncovered during all that earth moving. The terrain is perfect for golf, rippling fairways, humps and hollows. What's more, the course is always maintained in immaculate condition.

Situated just six miles from St Andrews, Kingsbarns is an important addition to the superb links courses in this area. It is feasible that this might be one of the last true links courses to be built along Scotland's coastline and if so, it is just as well that it's an absolute cracker and deserves to be bracketed alongside the greatest courses in the world.

David Scott – Professional writes:
Kingsbarns Golf Links is complemented by a dramatic seaside setting and a welcoming staff dedicated to the highest standards of service and comfort. The course offers sea views from every hole as the routing snakes along almost two miles of varying coastline. Sandy beaches, a rocky foreshore and the bay beyond Cambo Ness all reinforce the relationship Kingsbarns enjoys with the North Sea.

Kingsbarns strives to provide a golfing experience that is memorable for all the right reasons: the enjoyable classic links course itself, unique seaside vistas, and attention to golfers' needs by attentive staff members.

A heart-felt welcome awaits all golfers at Kingsbarns Golf Links.

Kevin Murray

ROYAL BIRKDALE GOLF CLUB
Waterloo Road, Birkdale, Southport, Merseyside, PR8 2LX, England
Telephone: +44 (0) 1704 567920
Website: www.royalbirkdale.com
Architect: George Low, F.W. Hawtree and J.H. Taylor
Visitors: Contact in advance - Not Sat

Average Reviewers' Score:

Reviewers' Comments

Royal Birkdale is quite rightly England's best course – nothing really comes near to it for a complete all round test... Brilliant Open venue with acres of space in and around the sandhills on the course... Every hole is a unique and interesting championship test... Very fair if you hit it straight... No weak holes, just a brilliant links course and a fair one too... Wonderful layout which tests golfers of all abilities... Dunes serve to frame the holes as you play around, but not over the dunes. This gives each hole a unique, almost isolated feel... Surprised by blind tee shots at the 9th and 16th holes – they still allow this in the modern era of Open venues, marvellous! Diabolically placed bunkers seem to threaten you on every shot, making proper club selection a difficult task... If you enjoy golf, and especially if you enjoy links golf, you owe it to yourself to play this magnificent track... I dream of playing golf here for the rest of my life! How can a course be any better?

Kevin Murray

Royal Birkdale is a famous links and widely recognised for its fairness. If you hit the fairways, rarely will the ball be thrown off course as the fairways are laid out in the flat-bottomed valleys between the towering dunes. These dunes, in turn, provide superb viewing platforms for spectators.

Birkdale has a superfluity of great golf holes. The 12th, a 183-yard par three is a classic hole and as natural as you can get. From a raised tee, the ball must carry across a hollow, whilst avoiding four deep pot bunkers before coming to rest on a narrow, raised green that is nestled at the feet of tussocky sand dunes. The par five 15th is Birkdale's longest hole and one of the most heavily bunkered on the course; knock it straight down the middle off the tee and then using a long iron or a fairway wood, avoid the bunkers spread-eagled across the fairway; chip it on and, bingo, an easy five!

The experience can be torrid when the wind is up, with white horses kicking and rearing their heads in the Irish Sea, crashing like kamikazes onto the beach. But whatever the weather, Royal Birkdale is a provocative place to play golf.

Brian G. Hodgkinson – Golf Professional writes:
'Tough but fair' may best describe Royal Birkdale.

Set amongst imposing sand dunes, it certainly has a completely natural feel that can be enjoyed by golfers of all abilities. From the daunting 1st hole to the unique setting of the famous 18th, which has set the scene for so many lasting and dramatic moments of past Ryder Cup matches and Open Championships, all players are challenged and encouraged to play their best golf ever.

For over 25 years, I have been greeting and meeting golfers from around the world. The overwhelming consensus is: 'if I could only play one course for the rest of my life, it would be Royal Birkdale'... a fitting tribute indeed.

Kevin Murray

Carnoustie (Championship)

CARNOUSTIE GOLF LINKS
Links Parade, Carnoustie, Angus, DD7 7JE, Scotland
Telephone: +44 (0) 1241 853789
Website: www.carnoustiegolflinks.co.uk
Architect: Old Tom Morris, James Braid
Visitors: Contact in advance - not Sat/Sun am

Average Reviewers' Score:

Reviewers' Comments

Carnoustie is without a doubt a beast... It is, frankly, the best layout I have ever played... There are no weak holes... and you need to think all the time... There are too many strategic features to note them all but it is a real true test of golf for any handicap... this is the real deal... it is not architecturally contrived, it is true golf... Every hole is a work of art... possibly the best bunkering on any golf course after Muirfield... The bunkers are as they should be: if you go in one, you drop a shot... So many great holes and absolutely no let-up... The greens are excellent, fast and true... As soon as you walk off the course you can 'think' your way back through the round and that is always a good sign... It's a course I respect but not one I necessarily enjoy, a bit like taking an exam... It will make you a better golfer and a stronger person... It is brutal if you leave your brain in the car park... Felt as though I had just gone 15 rounds with Mike Tyson after I putted out on 18... Put your ego aside and enjoy the test.

Darren Kirk - Scratch Design

Carnoustie is a big natural seaside links and one of the most difficult courses in the British Isles. Originally fashioned by Old Tom Morris and extended by James Braid in 1926, much has been written about Carnoustie over the years. The finishing holes are especially brutal and many consider that it has one of the greatest back nines in championship golf. Others will recall John Van de Velde's barefoot paddle in the Barry Burn at the 18th hole during the final round of the 1999 Open Championship, which ultimately lost him the title.

15, 16 and 17 are considered the world over to be three of golf's very best closing holes. "Lucky Slap", the 15th, is a 460-yard par four, where the fairway slopes from left to right into the path of two waiting bunkers and the approach shot must avoid a cluster of three bunkers sited to the right of the green.

The 17th is a complete conundrum, called "Island" because the Barry Burn snakes in front of the tee and then loops back, cutting across the fairway. Into the wind, it is tough to know what to do on this brutal par four.

Colin Sinclair – Head Professional writes:
Each time a golfer mentions Carnoustie, words such as tough, challenging and brutal spring to mind. After the 1999 Open Championship, the opinion was cemented that Carnoustie is the Mount Everest of golf courses. Personally, I think it's simply the finest layout of any links course in the world and it's a privilege to walk the superbly conditioned hallowed turf. It asks questions of the golfer and if you are unable to execute the shot correctly, you will be punished.

Carnoustie plays between 6,400 – 7,400 yards, depending on which tees you select. Burns and ditches meander their way through the course and accuracy off the tee is required on all holes with clever bunkering awaiting any errant shot. The greens – although not wide – are surprisingly long and typically links with subtle borrows which frequently fool golfers to read too much into their putts. Everything is laid out in front of you, no gimmicks and no hiding place. Carnoustie will find any weakness in your game but it will truly reward quality shots.

WOODHALL SPA GOLF CLUB
The Broadway, Woodhall Spa, Lincs, LN10 6PU, England
Telephone: +44 (0) 1526 352511
Website: www.woodhallspagolf.com
Architect: Harry Vardon, Harry Colt & Colonel S.V. Hotchkin
Visitors: Contact in advance - handicap certificate required

Average Reviewers' Score:

Reviewers' Comments

Simply the yardstick by which I will measure any other inland course, and frankly none that I have played so far come close... An inland golf course that is quite simply the best in the UK and one that would rival Pine Valley... Determinedly rugged in its beauty, lined with gorse and ragged bunkers... Very good in places but by no means the best... It lacks interest (in terms of elevation change)... It's long, tight, sandy and varied... No real drama holes... A heathland course that every other should aspire to... To me it seems contrived and its claim to fame must be the bunkers... Layout is demanding with some superb bunkers that look as though they were created by World War II bombers... I thought bunker comments may be exaggerated but their depth and difficulty is actually understated... Will expose even the best-disguised weakness in your game... Represents exceptional value if you are a member of any club affiliated to the EGU... Truly excellent in every way... If you love golf, you'll love Woodhall.

Woodhall Spa is an oasis in the heart of Lincolnshire. Set amongst glorious pine, birch and broom, this heathland course is an absolute delight to play. The sandy subsoil allows all-year-round golf, the springy turf making walking a real pleasure. Keep your ball in play and do your best to avoid the heather, gorse and bunkers.

The Hotchkin is bunker heaven (or hell), notorious for its deep, cavernous sand traps. It is also helpful if you can hit the ball long and straight. Otherwise you will be presented with some very tough second shots.

It is definitely worth making the trip to play this gem and the green fee is tremendous value for money too (especially if you are a member of an English golf club). And remember – the Hotchkin is undoubtedly one of the premier inland courses in the whole of the British Isles. Can you afford not to play it?

Richard A Latham – Director of Operations writes:
The Hotchkin Course at Woodhall Spa is generally regarded as one of the finest heathland courses in the world. In fact, it has been consistently rated in the world's top fifty over the last seventy years.

Long carries over heather, deep cavernous bunkers and a wonderful variety of short and long holes are the main features of the course. Interestingly, there are only three par 3s, ranging from 148 yards to 209 yards, and the penalties for an errant tee shot can be severe. The greens are relatively flat, although there are some subtle borrows, and they're in good order throughout the year. Most of the course is built on sand so this is an excellent winter course.

Ballybunion (Old)

BALLYBUNION GOLF CLUB
Sandhill Road, Ballybunion, County Kerry, Ireland
Telephone: +353 (0) 68 27146
Website: www.ballybuniongolfclub.ie
Architect: Jo McKenna, Lionel Hewson, Tom Simpson & Molly Gourlay
Visitors: Contact in advance – not at weekends

Average Reviewers' Score:

Reviewers' Comments
One of the great courses of the world… A golfer's paradise… A gem that deserves
all of the praise and accolades it has received… There are a couple of weak holes, but
the great holes and strong finish more than offset those… Every hole is outstanding
and a challenge in its own right… A pure test of links golf… From hole 7 until a pint
of Guinness, I don't think there is a better stretch of golf holes in the British Isles…
Overrated course… Simply loved this course… Found it somewhat disappointing… Best
course I have played in 30 years' golfing… Standing on the 7th tee is one of the most
memorable sights in my golf memory bank… Great golf course routing – like a great
novel – builds tension before releasing it, and the openers at Ballybunion do a great job
of this, with plenty of fun and challenge along the way… This area of the world is golfing
Mecca and nowhere does it more poignantly than Ballybunion… Magnificent.

The town of Ballybunion was named after the Bunion family, who owned the local 15th century castle. For many people, the name conjures up a vivid image of a wild links golf course on the edge of the Atlantic with fairways set amongst the gigantic duneland. Herbert Warren Wind, the distinguished American golf author, described Ballybunion as "nothing less than the finest seaside course I have ever seen".

As you drive from the historic town of Ballybunion, along the winding road to the golf course, your eyes feast upon the most spectacular links land imaginable. It will come as no surprise that this course, located on Sandhill Road, has some of the largest and most formidable sand dunes in Ireland.

The Old course is a thrilling challenge and if you are a very good golfer and there's a gentle breeze blowing, you might score well. If there's an onshore gale blowing, you are best to forget your score.

The layout is totally eccentric with a discarded architect's rulebook and just about anything goes. Each hole is refreshingly different and it builds from a rather ordinary start to a back nine crescendo with each homeward hole pitching and rolling through the windswept dunes. After playing the course it's likely that you will either fall into the like or loathe category, though nobody could argue that Ballybunion is unfair, nor could anybody deny that this amazing links course is totally in tune with Mother Nature.

James W. Finegan writes:
I want to go on record here as declaring the Old Course at Ballybunion to be the best seaside course I've ever played. There are two reasons for this conclusion. First, it seems to me to have more great holes than can legitimately be claimed by any of the other renowned links – and it has no poor holes. Second, for pure golfing pleasure – a combination, for me, of honest challenge, natural beauty, exhilaration, originality, and variety – I find it without equal.

Royal Dornoch (Championship)

ROYAL DORNOCH GOLF CLUB
Golf Road, Dornoch, Sutherland, IV25 3LW, Scotland
Telephone: +44 (0) 1862 810219
Website: www.royaldornoch.com
Architect: Old Tom Morris, John H. Taylor
Visitors: Contact in advance

Average Reviewers' Score:

Reviewers' Comments

Wow just about captures it! There's something mystical about Royal Dornoch... There's an X-factor, an intangible golfing variable that you feel from start to finish. You cannot describe what it is, but rest assured that it does exist and you can only experience it by playing! Holes have a great variety of twists, turns, and doglegs, and there is enough elevation change to give you the sense of never quite being able to find your balance or your game... Greens are like up-turned saucers... 2nd is a great par 3 with a green that repels all but the best shots... Stunning run of holes from 3-6 and an amazing feeling standing on the 9th tee... Slightly disappointed by the back nine... Back nine along that wonderful coastline is heaven... The most subtly difficult course I've played... With the gorse in bloom and the aquamarine sea ever-present, there can be no finer place on earth to play golf... You will be enchanted by the whole experience, honestly... A perfect links course... Pure theatrical magic.

Royal Dornoch Golf Club is spellbinding. It seems to mesmerise amateur and professional golfers from all over the world and many make the pilgrimage to this natural links at some point in their lives.

It's the timeless setting that makes Dornoch such a pleasing place to play golf. It's wild, isolated and, at the same time, absolutely beautiful; there's the blaze of colour in early summer when the gorse is in flower. The pure white sandy beach divides the links from the Dornoch Firth and it all feels very humbling.

Ostensibly, the course itself is pretty straightforward: it's an out-and-back layout. Many of the greens, though, are built on natural raised plateaux making approach play especially challenging. It's the raised domed greens that became the trademark of Dornoch's most famous son, Donald Ross.

Most people know about Royal Dornoch and many have this course on their must-play list. All we can say is that you shouldn't leave it too late, (as did Bernard Darwin) – this course must be played sooner rather than later. "And then, alas! – worst of all the deficiencies in my education – there is Dornoch. I never seem yet to have enough time or enough money to get so far north."

Andrew Skinner – Head Professional writes:
The remoteness of Royal Dornoch has helped create a mystique about this magnificent golfing outpost in the far north of Scotland. Situated just 4 degrees below the Arctic Circle, it is possible on a June evening to play golf until almost midnight.

The world's greatest golfers and golf writers have been lavish in their praise of Royal Dornoch. In a letter, Tom Watson thanked the club for the privilege of playing one of the world's truly great golf courses. He described the three rounds that he played during his first visit "as the most fun he had ever had playing golf".

In recent times, Royal Dornoch, with its panoramic views, natural, rolling and gorse-lined fairways, has been regularly ranked by illustrious golf panels among the world's Top 15 courses.

Lahinch (Old)

LAHINCH GOLF CLUB
Lahinch, County Clare, Ireland
Telephone: +353 (0) 65 7081 103
Website: www.lahinchgolf.com
Architect: Old Tom Morris, Dr Alister MacKenzie, John Burke, Martin Hawtree
Visitors: Contact in advance

Average Reviewers' Score:

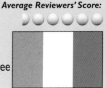

Reviewers' Comments

Top of the Irish Charts… Quite simply the best pure links course… It has everything… Brilliantly strategic… Blind shots, but each of the landing areas are expansive enough to keep them fair… Bunkering is fantastic… All of the greens brilliantly contoured except the par 5 18th which, in a stroke of exquisite simplicity, is pancake flat… Very traditional and typically Old Tom Morris… There are fast running fairways, beautiful dogleg par 4s with demanding tee shots, driveable par 4s and the quirky yet fascinating Klondyke and Dell… Should be famous for the best collection of par 4s in Ireland… Demands solid play, but is visually pleasing and, most of all, it is fun… Think links golf, think blind shots, pot bunkers, sea views, sweeping beaches, heavily undulating fairways and greens, Lahinch has the lot *and* goats! Routing is convoluted and bizarre… Has earned the nickname "The St Andrews of Ireland" for good reason… A course where I would love to be a member and play every day… Quintessential links golf… A golfer's paradise… Pure jazz.

Golf at Lahinch dates back to 1892. Three local Limerick golfers laid out an 18-hole course, assisted by officers of the Scottish "Black Watch" regiment who were stationed in Limerick at that time. In 1894, Old Tom Morris was commissioned to make improvements to the layout and he made excellent use of the natural terrain, especially the giant sand dunes. Old Tom believed that Lahinch was the finest natural course that he had seen.

This is an enchanting place to play golf. It's rugged, distinctive, unusually varied and immensely entertaining. It's a traditional out and back layout, situated next to the lovely beach of Liscannor Bay.

Views across the bay from the 4th are uplifting. This 428-yard par four has a blind drive to a hidden fairway and the approach to the green is obscured by a hill on the right. The 5th is a short par five named Klondyke. It's one of the most unusual holes in golf and an Old Tom speciality. The tee shot needs to find a narrow rippled fairway located in a valley between dunes. A blind second shot then has to negotiate Klondyke, a towering sand dune that straddles the fairway some 200 yards away from the green. It's certainly a quirky hole but it's also very memorable.

The Old course at Lahinch is an absolute gem. Take note of where the goats are. If they are sheltering near the clubhouse, take your umbrella – you are in for a wet round!

Donald Steel writes:
Described by Herbert Warren Wind as the St Andrews of Ireland, Lahinch is a small town on the Atlantic coast of County Clare which might be almost totally unknown were it not for the mountainous dune country lining the shore to provide the perfect medium for links golf. It is a spectacular example of the changing levels, hummocky dips and extravagant contours that architects strive in vain to introduce, and there is a whiff of whimsy about it which the Irish appreciate more than most.

Loch Lomond

LOCH LOMOND GOLF CLUB

Rossdhu House, Luss by Alexandria, Dunbartonshire, G83 8NT, Scotland
Telephone: +44 (0) 1436 655555
Website: www.lochlomond.com
Architect: Tom Weiskopf and Jay Morrish
Visitors: Members' guests only – course closed Nov-Mar

Average Reviewers' Score:

Reviewers' Comments

Without doubt the best golfing experience in the UK… This has got to be the best course that I will ever get the chance to play in my life… The scenery is breathtaking, even on a rainy day… The setting is stunning, the golf course superb and the scenery utterly breathtaking… Course is a tremendous challenge and tends to play longer than the card… Greens are amazing and fairways unchallenged by any other… 5th is a superb par three and the 18th a tremendous finishing hole… There are better courses but for an experience and day out there is no better… Most golfers from all over the world agree that Loch Lomond provides the best golfing experience… Staff are most genuine, friendly and helpful… What a tremendous experience… Please invite me back!

Graham Whitworth

It doesn't matter whether you take the high road or the low road, a visit to the bonnie banks o' Loch Lomond is a romantic experience.

Loch Lomond Golf Club is set in more than 600 acres of sheltered seclusion, sandwiched between the mountains and the historic lochside. The golf course contains two Sites of Special Scientific Interest – protecting rare plants and unusual woodland – and the site is designated as a National Scenic Area.

The course, designed by the successful Jay Morrish and Tom Weiskopf partnership, opened for play in 1993 to a fanfare. Weiskopf regards Loch Lomond as his "lasting memorial to golf" and who could argue with him? It's already a classic course and the long-term home to the Scottish Open. According to Colin Montgomerie, "wherever Loch Lomond is ranked, it ought to be higher".

Colin Campbell – Director of Golf writes:

Nestled at the foot of Ben Lomond sits the picturesque Loch Lomond Golf Club. Set in 660 acres of the Clan Colquhoun estate, Rossdhu House provides the ultimate clubhouse from which to begin your golfing experience.

The well manicured fairways and fast greens provide a fair test of golf to all golfers having the privilege to play at Loch Lomond. Flowering rhododendrons and an extensive range of wildlife add a beautiful backdrop. It's hard to believe that the club is only 20 minutes from Glasgow.

The 6th, a 625-yard par five, has a daunting tee shot with the loch stretching all the way up the right hand side of the hole. Even a good drive leaves a tough second shot having to negotiate a well-positioned bunker in the middle of the fairway. This sets up a tricky approach shot into a typical small green guarded by an old overhanging oak tree.

When you do eventually reach the 18th, you certainly can't afford a lapse in concentration. The long sweeping dogleg left round Rossdhu Bay can bring a grandstand finish to any level of golf. Many people attempt to bite off more than they can chew, resulting in the inevitable watery grave!

Waterville

WATERVILLE GOLF LINKS
Waterville, County Kerry, Ireland
Telephone: +353 (0) 66 947 4102
Website: www.watervillehouse.com
Architect: Claude Harmon, Eddie Hackett, Tom Fazio
Visitors: Contact in advance

Average Reviewers' Score:

Reviewers' Comments
Wow – what a course… Waterville was the highlight of our trip… Everything here is
spot on, variety, quality, twists and turns, history… Bunkering is penal and strategic and
the holes have a wonderful flow to them that gives a natural feel to the landscape…
Layout is nothing special… It is so overrated… Waterville seems to elicit a wide variety of
responses. Put me down as a fan and admirer of a great links golf course… Has a sterling
collection of par 4s that, in my mind, is rivalled only by Muirfield… 3rd hole is excellent;
I love the curve round the bay and the green seemingly hung out to dry… Variety in the
design has produced such diverse holes as the long 11th, all duck or no dinner par 3 12th,
dramatic 15th, 16th and 17th, and fine 18th… Payne Stewart statue is a fitting tribute
to a wonderful person… When I come back to this neck of the woods, I will head for
Waterville first and probably stay here… It's the best of the lot.

Waterville plays on a promontory surrounded by the sea. It's a stunning, remote location with views to the northeast of the Macgillycuddy's Reeks mountain range and to the southwest across the beautiful Ballinskelligs Bay and the Atlantic Ocean. The fairways are gently undulating, the front nine plays across relatively flat ground whilst the back nine weaves its way through avenues of tall dunes. The view from the elevated 17th tee, an excellent par 3 called "Mulcahy's Peak" after the founder Jack Mulcahy, is simply breathtaking.

There are few courses that can boast such a fine collection of unique and great golf holes. Waterville has three outstanding par threes and three excellent par fives, the par fours are pretty good too. The 11th is a heavenly short par five with a rippling fairway protected on both flanks by towering dunes. The 366-yard par four 16th was once called "Round the Bend" because it follows the natural curvature of the Atlantic coastline. It was here that Liam Higgins, the local pro, had a hole-in-one on his way to setting a course record of 65. Fittingly, the hole is now called "Liam's Ace".

The remoteness of the links has precluded it from hosting any big competitions, but famous golfers find their way here and they all leave with the feeling that it's a very special place.

Jay Connolly – Professional writes:
Waterville is a unique combination of classic linksland in a pristine remote setting. Surrounded by the Atlantic Ocean and the Inny River estuary, its beauty and challenge were recently enhanced by world-renowned architect, Tom Fazio. The front nine is highlighted by 3 holes bordering the estuary and the back nine with 3 finishing holes bordering the wild Atlantic.

The entire course is strong yet fair, and allows all the shots that define links golf. Waterville is maintained to world-class standards with firm and fast conditions and true and consistent greens. Various tee positions allow golfers of all skill levels to enjoy Waterville. By the way, the first hole is called 'Last Easy' which may explain why its membership includes three Open Champions!

Portmarnock (Old)

PORTMARNOCK GOLF CLUB
Portmarnock, County Dublin, Ireland
Telephone: +353 (0) 1 846 2968
Website: www.portmarnockgolfclub.ie
Architect: William Pickeman
Visitors: Welcome – see website for booking information

Average Reviewers' Score:

Reviewers' Comments

If you love golf, you have to play this course... How tough do you want your golf? What a tough course... The first thing you will notice about Portmarnock is its solitude. Being surrounded by water on three sides, the course stands isolated. Solitary trees stand arched back, humbled by the sea. They stand in testimony to the wind... Don't forget the waterproofs... A good links course with many very good golf holes... Very solid course... Holes are challenging, and fair, but lack distinguishing characteristics... It is the flatness of the course in my mind that is its enduring character and it's this prevalent feature that provides the course with its fairness... What a course! Tough, tough holes, a great finish and as everyone says, the last five are great, but so are all the holes... I love this course... Pro shop very friendly and helpful – wonderful people... If you are travelling over to play then pay the extra money to play Old Portmarnock over the Hotel links... If you get the chance, then play Portmarnock Old... It will test every part of your game.

Aidan Bradley

Portmarnock Golf Club is situated on its own sandy peninsula, approximately two miles long and covering some 500 acres. In 1893, William Pickeman, a Scottish insurance broker, and his friend George Ross, rowed across the sea from Sutton to the peninsular and immediately realised that this was prime golfing terrain. In those days, the peninsular could only be reached by boat.

Portmarnock is a natural links, and considered to be a very fair golf course. With water on three sides, the course is at the mercy of the wind. Laid out broadly in two loops of nine holes, you are invariably playing in different directions. Measuring over 7,300 yards from the back tees, it is a formidable test of golf and you will need your very best putting game because the greens are lightning fast and true.

There are superb views to the south of the Ireland's Eye (a small island), home to important seabird colonies and the Hill of Howth. On a clear day looking northwest, the Mountains of Mourne are visible. The closing five holes are especially brutal. The first of these closing holes, the 14th, requires an accurate approach shot to a narrow green, or in Joe Carr's case, an accurate drive. Apparently Carr, an amateur, made a hole-in-one on this 385-yard par four!

Joey Purcell – Head Professional – Portmarnock
Portmarnock is one of the world's greatest golf courses, surrounded by water on three sides. The club has played host to every important professional Irish golfing event, including 19 Irish Opens (12 between 1976 – 1990 and most recently in 2003) and we have also hosted all the top amateur events. In 1991, we were the first Irish club to host the Walker Cup and, in 2006, we once again hosted the Irish Amateur Championship.

To keep up with modern technology and player demands, we are constantly improving the links and we have recently upgraded the bunkers and tees. We're very aware of the need to maintain this world famous course to a very high standard, not only for our 1,300 members, but also for the 7,500 plus golfers who visit each year to savour the unique Portmarnock experience.

Portmarnock Golf Club founded in 1894 is one of the top links courses in the world. The club has hosted the Walker Cup, Amateur Championship – Men's & Ladies – and many Professional tournaments including 18 Irish Opens. The course has all the essential ingredients of true links golf; fast plateau greens superb bunkering and a truly memorable mix of par 3s 4s and 5s.

A "must play" course on any discerning golfer's list.

Aidan Bradley

ROYAL LIVERPOOL GOLF CLUB
Meols Drive, Hoylake, Wirral, Merseyside, CH47 4AL, England
Telephone: +44 (0) 151 632 3101
Website: www.royal-liverpool-golf.com
Architect: George Morris, Harry Colt, Donald Steel
Visitors: Not Thu am or weekends – contact in advance

Average Reviewers' Score:

Reviewers' Comments

Had the ultimate privilege of playing Hoylake four days after the Open and couldn't have asked for more… It's a supreme test of golf… Played here recently on the back of the return of the Open Championship to follow in the footsteps of the best… I have never before and probably never will putt on truer greens… Some would say it's flat and boring and I'd agree with flat but boring it certainly isn't… Are there many dunes? No. Does it matter? Definitely not… Really enjoyed the course and it was a decent test – inevitable wind and deep bunkers are really tricky… The wind and the deep bunkers are plenty to deal with and it is easy to run up some big scores… Bring your A game or you will be in trouble… There are some genuinely stunning holes on this course and the 10th and 11th stand out for me… Had a go at holing out from 190 yards on the 14th like Tiger did, guess what I missed! The 17th is one of my favourites and is a tough par four… This course is as good a test of your inner game as any I have come across.

The Open Championship finally returned to Royal Liverpool in 2006 after a 39-year gap. Hoylake, as it is called by those in the know, has a long and illustrious history of playing host to the Open, and has now hosted eleven, its first in 1897. Founded in 1869, Hoylake is the second oldest seaside links course in England – only Royal North Devon is the more senior.

Donald Steel was commissioned to make alterations to the course ahead of the Open; these changes included a number of new greens, tees and bunkers. Work was completed in 2001 and Hoylake now stretches out in excess of 7,000 yards.

The land is unusually flat, offering little in the way of definition. Houses border three sides of the course and the Dee Estuary lies on the western side. When you get out onto the course, the undulations become more pronounced and, as you move away from the houses, the overall aesthetic improves. The holes alongside the shore (9th, 10th, 11th and 12th) are the most visually appealing and very challenging.

Without doubt, Royal Liverpool is a tough links. Only a couple of holes are in the dunes – otherwise there is little protection from the ever-changing wind. There is nothing artificial about the course. It represents a traditional, genuine test of golf and it was heart-warming to see that Hoylake examined the very best players in 2006. They came, they saw and Tiger conquered!

Donald Steel writes:
The last word belongs to Tom Simpson and the obituary which, by mutual agreement, Henry Longhurst wrote before Simpson's death. In discussing some of his philosophies about golf course architecture, Simpson declared that, to be any good, a golf course must have out-of-bounds. "I take it you regard Hoylake as the finest in England," enquired Longhurst.

"Without any doubt," came the unhesitating reply.

Royal St George's

ROYAL ST GEORGE'S GOLF CLUB
Sandwich, Kent, CT13 9PB, England
Telephone: +44 (0) 1304 613090
Website: www.royalstgeorges.com
Architect: William Laidlaw Purves, Frank Pennink
Visitors: Contact in advance - not at the weekend

Average Reviewers' Score:

Reviewers' Comments

A real must for any golfer… Price was a bit steep but I didn't care, I just wanted to hit a drive over the monster bunkers at the 4th… You can see traces of the relentless wind… As usual, the links wind will be the biggest challenge with some par 4s being 3-shotters and the two par 5s in range when it is behind… Lots of pot bunkers… Land in any of the fairway bunkers and it's a dropped shot… Firm greens and terrific fairways… Lots of up and down on the fairways and blind tee shots… Apart from having wonderful greens and a few innovative bunkers, this is not worth the money… Magic bunkering around the greens… Greens are absolutely huge, hard and fast… No real signature hole, except maybe the 4th… 10th is probably the hardest par four on the course… Old-fashioned golf and real fun too… You may be good enough to score better than the winner of the first Open held here… Great history, great tradition – must be played.

In 1887, the course opened for play and was named "St George's" after the English patron saint. After only seven years of play, in 1894, Sandwich hosted its first of 13 Open Championships. This was the first Open to be played outside Scotland.

The course is not a traditional out and back layout. In a similar style to Muirfield, each nine is broadly circular, a loose figure of eight. There is nothing artificial about Royal St George's; there is a natural look and feel to the course that blends beautifully into the surroundings, with wild flowers, dune grasses and the sweet song of the lark. Commanding views over Pegwell Bay and the white cliffs of Dover ensure an amazing experience.

Royal St George's has some unique features; thatched roof shelters, the red cross of St George on the flags, and that bunker on the 4th hole cut into a huge dune, the UK's tallest and deepest bunker.

Andrew Brooks – Head Professional writes:
My advice for those playing Royal St George's for the first time is to always aim at the middle of the greens and ignore pin placement. Being patient will pay dividends – this was certainly the case for Ben Curtis when he won the 2003 Open Championship. I gave him some advice about the nuances of our course, including not to over borrow whilst putting. The rest is history.

My favourite holes include the 4th, where the bunker must be avoided at all costs with your tee shot. The par 3, 6th has a wonderful undulating green which is a fantastic putting surface and the tee shot at 14th is a real test with OOB all the way down the right hand side. The par 3 16th holds different memories – Tony Jacklin had the first televised hole-in-one here and Thomas Bjorn took three to escape the greenside bunker, waving goodbye to the 2003 Claret Jug in the process – if only he had have aimed for the middle of the green!

But my favourite shot must be the approach to the 8th hole with a mid iron when the pin is at the back of the green. I can assure you that you'll find a wonderful links experience waiting at Royal St George's.

THE EUROPEAN CLUB
Brittas Bay, Co Wicklow, Ireland
Telephone: +353 (0) 404 47415
Website: www.theeuropeanclub.com
Architect: Pat Ruddy
Visitors: Book in advance

Average Reviewers' Score:

Reviewers' Comments

One of the most interesting and most exciting links courses I've ever had the pleasure to play… A touch of Ballybunion and a hint of the Glashedy course at Ballyliffin awake the senses… We were expecting a great course and were not disappointed… I found the layout, routing and overall quality of the holes very mediocre… There are probably no weak holes, but the 7, 8, 10, 14, 17 and 18 are really great… 120-yard green on the 12th adds nothing to an already exceptional golf hole… Several fine holes on the back nine, bordering the Irish Sea… Layout pitches and rolls through and across some fabulous ground and the best holes hug Brittas Bay… This gem of a course provides the golfer with a stern test of accuracy and links technique… This course has a soul that is so often lost on today's courses… Much better than the more famous Portmarnock Old… It was really hard, but it was so much fun… Pat Ruddy must be commended… Hats off to the Ruddys.

The European Club is located in the garden of Ireland, between the coastal towns of Wicklow and Arklow, about 30 miles south of Dublin. It's Pat Ruddy's creation and he and his family have stayed there ever since. It's a unique experience, a 20-hole links set amongst rugged dunes and it opened for play in 1993 with only one thing missing – history.

This is an inspiring place for golf, huge dunes provide tremendous definition and the Irish Sea is very much a backcloth. It's a bit of a monster too; the 18-hole layout stretches to more than 7,000 yards, a challenging par 71. Two par 3s (7a & 12a) make up the par 77 20-hole layout and they are definitely worth playing, making a refreshing break from tradition.

Many of the holes are varied and capture one's attention and there are some great holes too. The 7th (stroke index 1) is a long 470-yard par four set on a sandbank that runs through a bed of reeds. A burn runs along the right hand side, beyond which there's a hundred acres of unspoiled land without a building to be seen. On the left are towering dunes, a marsh filled with reeds and more sand dunes by the green. Brittas Bay shimmers behind the green.

Pat Ruddy – architect of The European Club writes:
The links has been designed and is continually improved with modern championship play and rampant technology in mind. For example, it has grown from just over 6,700 yards on opening in 1992 to 7,358 yards today. Bunkering and green shaping have been given constant attention and the quest for perfection will go on in perpetuity.

The winners of over 40 major titles, including links record holder Tiger Woods, have visited to play golf and to study and talk golf course design. The European Club, thus, sits as a golfing crossroads for the world and it is usually so uncrowded that the cry of Fore! comes as a distinct shock.

The club is pleased with constant high rankings which seem to indicate that it is heading in the right direction.

Sunningdale (Old)

SUNNINGDALE GOLF CLUB
Ridgemount Road, Sunningdale, Berkshire, SL5 9RR, England
Telephone: +44 (0) 1344 621681
Website: www.sunningdale-golfclub.co.uk
Architect: Willie Park Junior, Harry Colt
Visitors: Contact in advance - Not Fri, Sat, Sun or public hols

Average Reviewers' Score:

Reviewers' Comments

One of the finest inland courses in GB&I... Play the Old before all others on your list of courses to play... 36 holes on the Old and the New at Sunningdale takes some beating... The Old is my favourite with a little more room off the tee and "big" greens... The turf is gorgeous and it's a course that is pleasing on the eye... This is real golf in a sublime setting where the staff take time for the visitor... Is the Old better than the New? It's like comparing rugby and football... This classic layout is very tight off the tee with heather and pine trees bordering every fairway... Enjoy that drive on the elevated 10th tee... Gets very busy in summer... It's pretty expensive to play here but it's cheaper than Wentworth and in my book Sunningdale is better... If I had to play one golf course only for the rest of my life – it would be a tough call – but I would say Sunningdale Old course.

The Old course at Sunningdale is one of the British Isles' most aesthetically pleasing inland courses. Lined with pine, birch and oak trees, it is a magnificent place to play golf. The emblem of the club is the oak tree, no doubt modelled on the huge specimen tree standing majestically beside the 18th green. It's incredible to believe that originally the golf course was laid out on barren, open land.

If you have already played the Old course, you will surely remember the elevated 10th tee, a fabulous driving hole and one of our all-time favourite holes. By the time you have putted out on the 10th, you will be ready for refreshments at the excellent halfway hut that sits welcomingly behind the green. What sheer delight!

Many people regard Sunningdale as the perfect golfing venue. The Old and New courses taken together are probably the finest pair of golf courses anywhere. On a sunny autumn day, walking on that perfect heathland turf, surely there is nowhere better to play golf with a few friends.

Keith Maxwell – Head Professional writes:
Sunningdale's Old and New courses sit side by side and provide two very different tests of golf.

The Old is much more tree-lined but still very much the heathland course it always has been. The layout is such that it allows the players to ease into the round with the opening holes being a fairly open par five followed by a tough par four, a short par four and uphill par three.

It is at this point that we appreciate the true beauty of Sunningdale as the 5th and 6th are set before us end to end. The 10th hole remains everyone's favourite; it's both eye catching and tough with the added bonus of our famous halfway hut. The closing holes very much epitomise Sunningdale with the backdrop of the double oak and Clubhouse.

Royal Lytham & St Annes

ROYAL LYTHAM & ST ANNES GOLF CLUB

Average Reviewers' Score:

Links Gate, St Annes on Sea, Lancashire, FY8 3LQ, England
Telephone: +44 (0) 1253 724206
Website: www.royallytham.org
Architect: Harry Colt, Herbert Fowler, Tom Simpson & C.K.Cotton
Visitors: Mon & Thu - Contact in advance

Reviewers' Comments

One word to describe the Lytham experience – *fantastic*! Had a wonderful experience, members were the most welcoming of all Open venues… Their 94-year-old Dormy house – it is a *must*… Honestly, this was *by far* the best golfing experience I have ever had… Fairly flat and uninteresting with very few memorable holes… Fantastic links course that asks all the right questions… A tough golf course – long, tight and relentless… Strategic bunkering, tricky and slick greens and a brutal closing stretch… 8th hole was my favourite; played to a raised green at the corner of the course… It gets relatively tight around the turn… Bunkers are deep and plentiful round the whole estate so don't expect to keep your sand wedge in the bag… Only letdown is the lack of sea views, otherwise it's as good as it gets… Staff were exceptionally welcoming… You owe it to yourself as a golfer to tread the same turf as Seve… Fantastic experience!

Jim McCann

Royal Lytham & St Annes is the most northerly of the English championship links courses, situated only 10 miles, as the seagull flies, from its illustrious neighbour, Royal Birkdale.

The links is positioned – rather unusually – surrounded by red brick houses and flanked on the west by the railway line while the guardian Victorian clubhouse watches sternly over the course. The conditioning of the course is exceptional and not as rough and ready as many of its contemporaries. The ground is relatively even, except perhaps on a couple of holes, where the land is slightly wrinkled.

The course itself is extremely tough, only Carnoustie (on the British Open circuit) is thought to be tougher. The greens are firm, fast and true and the 1st is unique because this is the only par three starting hole on the Open Championship circuit and it's a long one, measuring 206 yards from the back tees.

The Professional Team of Eddie Birchenough, Simon Avery, Ben Squires and Tim Rich writes:
At first sight, Royal Lytham & St Annes Golf Club doesn't strike one as a classic links, with neither sight nor sound of the sea. Despite being one of the shorter courses on the Open rota, Lytham retains its place as one of the most demanding due to its tight fairways, deep rough and 200 strategically placed bunkers.

Requiring accurate ball striking and a delicate short game, it is no surprise this course has crowned many great champions. From Seve Ballesteros prevailing over Nick Price on a glorious Monday in 1988 to Gary Player's left handed chip from the side of the clubhouse to claim victory in 1974. However, Royal Lytham probably remains most famous of all for Bobby Jones's miraculous second shot from the sandy wasteland on the left of the 17th to help snatch the Claret Jug from Al Watrous in 1926.

Set on a narrow strip of land amongst Lytham's red brick homes, the course may make no claim to being the prettiest of championship venues. However, as a supreme test of a golfer's all round skill, its position is assured at the very top of the list.

Cédric Hannedouche

Ganton

GANTON GOLF CLUB
Ganton, North Yorkshire, YO12 4PA, England
Telephone: +44 (0) 1994 710329 **Website:** www.gantongolfclub.com
Architect: Tom Chisholm, James Braid, Ted Ray, J.H. Taylor,
Alister MacKenzie, Tom Simpson and C.K. Cotton
Visitors: Via prior arrangement – not at weekends

Average Reviewers' Score:

Reviewers' Comments

Ganton is so understated, so subtle – apart from its bunkering… My favourite inland course… Probably the greatest inland course with links style in the world… A combination of links land in a heathland setting… Have never played a course and had to use my sand wedge so often – bunkers are so strategically placed (and often enormous) that you will do very well to go round here and avoid them… Need to be long and very straight. If you see your ball going toward the ever-present gorse, it is in the gorse… Every hole is a true challenge – even the short par 4 14th… Like all true classic courses, holes change direction all the way round and there are a couple of delightful surprises at the end thrown in for good measure… A real test, even for long hitters… The championship pedigree is exceptional… Any golfer who is serious about playing the great courses of the British Isles must play Ganton… Very friendly members… Rightly rated as highly as this… Well worth the trip.

To classify Ganton as a heathland course is a misnomer – one could just as easily categorise it as an inland links, as it's situated in the rural Vale of Pickering, nine miles from the sea. This sandy, gently undulating site was once a North Sea inlet. Consequently, it has all the characteristics of a links and a heathland course. Either way, it's a perfect place to play golf.

The bunkering is quite extraordinary, a real feature of the course. With over 100 cunningly placed bunkers, some of which are simply huge, both in breadth and in depth, whilst others are small. Only lucky (or very good golfers) will avoid the sand traps at Ganton.

If you blend the Old course at Walton Heath with Woodhall Spa's Hotchkin course and then throw in a touch of Muirfield, you've got Ganton. Occupying open, windswept heathland, it's a supreme thinking man and woman's test of golf; the fast greens and firm fairways test the very best players. Various types of thick gorse, heather and broom highlight the course during the spring and summer months.

Ganton is a friendly club that opens its doors warmly to visitors (providing you have a handicap). If you are a serious golfer and have never played here, we strongly recommend it.

James W. Finegan writes:
Playing Ganton is a starkly confrontational business. Hole after hole, shot after shot, without so much as a moment's let-up, it is golfer versus golf course. Never is there a free swing, where we can open the shoulders, "grip it and rip it." Always, catastrophe lurks, in either the sandy caverns or the great stands of gorse. At times we incline to believe that the entire course must have been dredged up out of a sea of gorse, an intractable expanse of potentially unplayable – and literally prickly – lies. As for the bunkers, 123 by actual count – many of them malevolently deep, their banks often gorse infested, some pits with revetted faces, a few with boarded faces, certain bunkers requiring steps in order to get in and out – these hazards fiercely stare us down at every turn.

Cédric Hannedouche

Wentworth (West)

WENTWORTH CLUB
Virginia Water, Surrey, GU25 4LS, England
Telephone: +44 (0) 1344 842201
Website: www.wentworthclub.com
Architect: Harry Colt and Ernie Els
Visitors: Handicap certificate required – contact in advance

Average Reviewers' Score:

Reviewers' Comments

Wentworth is entertainment for any golfer playing well or badly… The whole place has a buzz… A lovely place to play golf and certainly has a bit of X-factor… It's not the best in the country (it's not the best in the surrounding area), but you do get half way around and think, "Wow, this is Wentworth"… Expensive – but worth every penny… Expensive it is, but that's probably what sets it apart in the desirability stakes… Recent changes made by Ernie Els will need some time to settle in but the West has certainly been toughened up and tightened up… Water at the 8th is now a real problem cutting all the way around the green… A fantastic design and, without doubt, it is a classic but there are better heathland courses in the area… Recommend playing in winter, it's cheaper… I really enjoyed it and will be returning again shortly… Great course, great atmosphere, great experience… Wentworth scores very highly on ambience… Loved every minute… One of my all-time favourites.

Kevin Murray

The West course at Wentworth is the most famous of the Surrey heath and heather courses and is also the most televised course in Britain. Designed in 1926 by Harry Colt, it's a relative youngster in the scheme of things as many of Surrey's famous sand-belt courses were established around the turn of the 19th century.

When you step onto the first tee, you will feel an overwhelming sense of familiarity. It is definitely a place most people would be more than happy to call home and play the monthly medal here for the rest of their lives. The holes weave their way through sprinklings of heather and across gently undulating terrain. Mature oaks, pines and silver birch trees line each and every fairway.

This is a truly classy golf course and it's a tough one too, especially after Ernie Els gave the West a new set of teeth in 2006. It now measures more than 7,300 yards from the tips. With 30 new bunkers and some stunning new tees, the Burma Road is now a serious 21st century challenge.

Ernie Els writes:
Everyone knows how much I love the West Course at Wentworth. I just have so many great memories from the tournaments I've played here over the years. This is also the place that we choose to call home. It's a wonderful part of the world to live, with everything we could ever want on our doorstep.

It's a great privilege for me, then, to be given the opportunity to refine and modernise the West Course. The brief was not to change the character of the golf course. That would be a crime! But to ensure it remains a fitting challenge for the professional who plays in the tournaments, as well as the amateur golfer.

The fact is the West Course did not play as Harry Colt intended and the changes address that. I needed to ensure that amateurs can still enjoy the course for what it is – a great piece of golf course design. After all, for 50 weeks of the year, it is amateurs who play this golf course. But for the other two weeks of the year, when the prestigious tournaments come to town, I think it's important this great old golf course remains a test for the best.

WALTON HEATH GOLF CLUB

Deans Lane, Walton on the Hill, Surrey, KT20 7TP, England
Telephone: +44 (0) 1737 812380
Website: www.whgc.co.uk
Architect: Herbert Fowler
Visitors: Contact in advance - weekends limited

Average Reviewers' Score:

Reviewers' Comments

I love Walton Heath – either course – but the Old is special, very special... Outside of the British Open courses I've not been to a club steeped in as much history... Lovely course that is pure and simple heathland... Has all the attributes that you would expect from great courses – natural layout out, strategic bunkering, penal rough, heather, and a varied selection of holes and of course firm and true greens... Opens up to a poor start with an average 1st hole, cross the road and it soon opens up... Challenging long par 4s, well guarded par 3s and par 5s you cannot attack without perfect placement off the tee... Some of the holes felt quite cramped... Sensational greens, great fairways, tough bunkers – ooh and don't forget the heather, but do your best to avoid it! I enjoyed the whole experience and it was followed up by a stellar lunch... Has one of the most charming putting greens you will ever see... Play Walton Heath for all that is good about English heathland golf.

Walton Heath Golf Club

Walton Heath is where links golf meets inland golf. There is no salty whiff of sea air, but the course plays and feels like a seaside links. A profusion of heather stripes the edge of the fairways. In the summer, when the heather is in flower, it is an absolute delight to look at, but a real challenge to play out of. The greens are true and fast and the undulations make it tough to read the lines and the pace of putts.

This is a course that favours the lower handicap golfer. Some of the carries across the heather are quite lengthy and if you don't hit the fairways, you can often wave goodbye to your ball. There are some really strong holes on the Old course – one of the best of the outward nine is the 5th, a cracking 391-yard par four that demands a solid drive that must avoid the thick, tangly heather shrouding the fairway. A mid-iron approach shot will find the green, amply guarded by bunkers left and right. The last three holes are especially challenging, especially the 16th, a 510-yard par five.

Walton Heath has hosted many important competitions, not least the 1981 Ryder Cup. Unfortunately, Europe was thrashed 9½ - 18½ by America, thanks to the likes of Watson and Nicklaus. For serious golfers, this is a fantastic venue for a golf day and lunch is simply stunning.

Ken Macpherson – Professional writes:

"A links course laid out inland" was how the Old Course was described in 1904 and its layout is very similar to The Old Course at St Andrews in that is eight holes out, a loop of three, and seven holes back.

The firm, closely-cut turf is ideal for the run-up approach shot and the design of the course, together with the ever-present wind, encourages this style of old fashioned golf.

Although the course is a long one, the fast fairways produce additional run provided that they can be found off the tee. Few courses anywhere can lay claim to the description "A driver's course" more than Walton Heath.

Stuart Abramson

Royal Troon (Old)

ROYAL TROON GOLF CLUB
Craigend Road, Troon, Ayrshire, KA10 6EP, Scotland
Telephone: +44 (0) 1292 311555
Website: www.royaltroon.com
Architect: George Strath, Willie Fernie & James Braid
Visitors: May to Oct, Mon, Tue & Thu only. Book in advance

Average Reviewers' Score:

Reviewers' Comments

I really have enjoyed my rounds at Troon… Somewhat disappointing when compared to the other courses on the Open rota… Course in my view is really good, but not great… I fear its length may endanger the chances of it staying on the rotation… Found this a really enjoyable quality links… Overall, a pretty uninspiring course to play… Change of atmosphere around holes 7-9 (slight move in from the coast), three top quality holes though; including the Postage Stamp… Best holes are reserved for the middle of your round when there are some nice changes in elevation between the 6th and 12th holes… A pleasure to play the Postage Stamp – though the green didn't seem that small (still missed it, of course)… Front nine played downwind and it was head down for the back nine into the prevailing wind… Troon comes in for some overly harsh criticism…
A pleasure to add an Open championship course to my played list and Troon for me was a great experience… I would certainly like to come back.

Royal Troon Golf Club remains the first (and last) club in Great Britain to have been granted Royal status under the long reign of Queen Elizabeth II.

It's a traditional out and back links course and the opening few holes are relatively gentle, with a series of short par fours running along the Firth of Clyde. It's from these early holes that you get the chance to soak up the views. On a clear day, you can see the distant Ailsa Craig in the south, and to the west, the majestic mountains on the Isle of Arran.

The course measures 7,150 yards from the back tees but line is more important than distance from the tee. Bunkers are everywhere, the majority of which are not visible from the tees. There's plenty of deep rough and a smattering of gorse and broom to punish the wayward shot. Make your score on the outward nine holes; the inward holes are severe, often playing into the prevailing northwesterly wind.

The following passage was published in Henry Cotton's Guide to Golf In The British Isles and was written by Troon's Professional for 17 years, William J Henderson, who died in 1970, the year after Sir Henry's book was published:

Troon Golf Club was founded in 1878 and we now have two courses, as well as a children's course and a good practice ground.

The greens are full of subtle borrows, not large, and the bunkers have a big catchment area. The most difficult hole is the 11th on the Old Course, where the tee shot line is between a steep rough sandhill and a big patch of whins and has the green touching the wall of the railway line. Jack Nicklaus ruined his Open chances with a 10 at this hole in 1962.

Cruden Bay

CRUDEN BAY GOLF CLUB
Aulton Road, Cruden Bay, Aberdeenshire, AB42 0NN, Scotland
Telephone: +44 (0) 1799 812285
Website: www.crudenbaygolfclub.co.uk
Architect: Old Tom Morris, Archie Simpson, Tom Simpson, Herbert Fowler
Visitors: Welcome weekdays – advisable to contact in advance

Average Reviewers' Score:

Reviewers' Comments

Cruden Bay is for all golfers with a soul… Course makes use of the natural terrain to wonderful and sometimes quirky effect… It's simply a delight… Whoever says this course is overrated, obviously takes their golf too seriously… There are dunes, fast running holes, significant elevation changes, driveable par 4s and, of course, blind shots… Has some blind shots but they are not contrived… It has every different aspect of links golf in one place… Some par fours are deceptively short, but the course has one of the hardest runs of links holes in golf… Course tests every facet of your game… View from the 11th tee is stunning, but the entire course has a great feel and ambience to it… One of my most enjoyable rounds… 9-hole St Olaf course is also a gem… Very friendly welcoming staff… Play here in late autumn when it's nearly deserted and I defy any golfer not to get in touch with his or her inner self… This is why you love this mad game.

Originally, Old Tom Morris was commissioned by the Great North of Scotland railway company to design the course at Cruden Bay and it opened for play in 1899. The railway company used pink granite to build a luxurious hotel, which was nicknamed "the Palace in the Sandhills". They hoped for the same success as at Gleneagles, but sadly, in 1952, the hotel was demolished. Money was tight in the 1950s and the club and course almost fell by the wayside until three local businessmen stepped in to save Cruden Bay from extinction.

Cruden Bay is an inspirational golf course, regarded by some as quirky and considered by others as a masterpiece. Either way, this is a thrilling place to play golf because the designers used the original lie of the land to fantastic effect.

Rugged linksland, pebble-dashed with sand dunes as high as three-storey buildings. Elevated tees cut high into the dunes, humped and hollowed fairways bumping their way along to punchbowl greens, nestling in attractive dells. And all set against the backdrop of the steely North Sea.

Winding its way in a figure of eight through towering dunes. Many of the holes are framed by the sandhills, enabling that wonderful feeling of intimacy. There are panoramic sea views, a stunning beach, driveable par fours, blind drives, back-to-back par threes.

Robbie Stewart – Head Professional writes:
Cruden Bay offers the golfer an opportunity to sample true links golf with one objective in mind – to enjoy the experience.

Compared to other traditional links courses, Cruden Bay is on the short side at less than 6,400 yards, but what it lacks in distance it makes up for with some spectacular views over the Bay of Cruden and a tremendous variety of holes, all of which are hugely interesting.

In common with all links courses, the wind plays a big part, adding to the fun and asking a different set of questions of the visiting golfer. This is a classic Old Tom Morris/Tom Simpson design which can be enjoyed equally by all standards of players.

Aidan Bradley

ROYAL PORTHCAWL GOLF CLUB

Rest Bay, Porthcawl, Mid Glamorgan, CF36 3VW, Wales
Telephone: +44 (0) 1656 782251
Website: www.royalporthcawl.com
Architect: Charles Gibson, Harry Colt, Tom Simpson,
Visitors: Contact in advance – weekdays only

Average Reviewers' Score:

Reviewers' Comments

Undoubtedly the finest course west of the Severn Bridge… One of the best I've ever played… A friendly welcome from the Pro shop helped… All very classy, interesting and varied… Lovely sea views with a nice low-key sort of feel to the place… Windy, long with greens like glass… The best three starting holes on a golf course worldwide… The finest set of par 3s I've yet to come across on any course… Hardly a weak hole, truly spectacular bunkering and superb greens… No stunning holes but no poor ones either… They have recently extended the 12th hole which is now even more challenging… Only grumble is that there was insufficient sand in the bunkers… The walk down the hill to the 18th green will lift the spirits… A subtle course that grows on you… Wonderfully quirky old wooden clubhouse… Where else can you order your sandwich by phone? Traditional golf course deserving to be in Britain's Top 10… Everyone visiting Wales should play a round at this marvellous golf course.

Royal Porthcawl Golf Club is located off the beaten track, east of Swansea and west of Cardiff. Despite being the highest ranked course in Wales, it remains relatively undiscovered.

Porthcawl was granted its royal title in 1909 by King Edward VII. Over the years, the layout has been extensively modified, most notably by Harry Colt in 1913 and then by Tom Simpson in 1933.

The first four holes and the last six holes represent classic links golf and the holes in the middle rise up onto higher ground, offering fantastic views across the Bristol Channel. It's not a long track at a little over 6,600 yards from the back tees, but it's a very subtle course where position from the tee is more important than distance. Gary Wolstenholme will vouch for this. Wolstenholme played Tiger Woods in the 1995 Walker Cup and despite being constantly out-driven by Woods, Wolstenholme controlled and positioned the ball better and secured a famous victory at the last hole.

The Bristol Channel acts as a funnel for Atlantic gales and the course is fully exposed to the wind. It's not a traditional out and back layout the holes loop back on one another, playing in various directions. With an absence of trees and dunes, the wind plays a powerful role.

Donald Steel writes:
Some seaside courses, hidden behind houses or dunes, might be thought guilty of a breach of the Trades Descriptions Act. It is a nice point whether sight of the sea is implied by definition but at Royal Porthcawl there are no possible doubts. It is unique in that the sea is in full view from every single hole.

Fredrik Liliedahl

GLENEAGLES HOTEL
Auchterarder, Perthshire, PH3 1NF, Scotland
Telephone: +44 (0) 1764 662231
Website: www.gleneagles.com
Architect: James Braid, Major C.K. Hutchinson and Donald Matheson
Visitors: Book at least 8 weeks in advance

Average Reviewers' Score:

Reviewers' Comments

I can unreservedly recommend the King's course to anyone… Am a big fan of James Braid and this course is a masterpiece… Lovely track, but not as good as I had hoped for… Views are superb and the layout is interesting and challenging… Played to the sternest par of 68 that one could imagine… Rambles through rolling terrain and presents one great challenge after another… Get the first hole out of the way and it seems that you have the course to yourself… Great mix of long and short holes and a very memorable finish… Only played the King's once but can remember almost every hole with clarity and fondness… Real stand-out holes for me were the 3rd, 7th and 15th but the rest were not far behind… A lovely place to be – even if you're not golfing – especially on a summer evening… My trouble is I can't decide if I like this more than the Queen's course. Play both before you die… Pay the money and get up there is my advice.

Anthony Munter

Gleneagles is the perfect mountain setting for a game of golf and the King's course is surely the best moorland track in the world. The sweeping views of the Ochil Hills and the peaks of Ben Vorlich and the Trossachs are simply ravishing.

Braid was given the most perfect terrain upon which to build a golf course and he built a very special golf course. The holes blend perfectly into the landscape. The springy fairways wind their way through punishing rough, strewn with heather and gorse. Many mature pines, silver birch and rowan provide natural amphitheatres on a number of the holes.

You cannot help but be enchanted by this golf course. Even the named holes are evocative: Silver Tassie, Blink Bonnie and Wee Bogle. But it's the views that will probably interrupt your concentration on the game.

A number of important events have been played over the King's course, including the Curtis Cup, Dunhill Trophy, Scottish Open and the WPGA Championship of Europe. Lee Trevino, standing on the 1st tee of the King's course, remarked:"If heaven is as good as this, I sure hope they have some tee times left".

Russell Smith – Head Professional writes:

The King's course at Gleneagles is a masterpiece of design. It was the designer James Braid's plan to test even the best players' shot-making skills over eighteen holes. Selecting the right club for each approach shot is the secret on the King's.

It is one of the most beautiful and exhilarating places to play golf in the world, with the springy moorland turf underfoot, the sweeping views from the tees all around, the rock faced mountains to the north, the green hills to the south and the peaks of the Trossachs and Ben Vorlich on the western horizon. The finishing 18th hole is a classic. One of the best feelings in golf is a well-struck drive over the saddle that can set up a birdie or even an eagle... what a finish that would be!

Anthony Munter

Prestwick

PRESTWICK GOLF CLUB
2 Links Road, Prestwick, Ayrshire, KA9 1QG, Scotland
Telephone: +44 (0) 1292 671020
Website: www.prestwickgc.co.uk **Architect:** Old Tom Morris
Visitors: Contact in advance – restrictions Thu and Sun, no visitors
Sat or Public Holidays

Average Reviewers' Score:

Reviewers' Comments

'Birthplace of The Open', need I say more? The gem on my Scotland tour… A real golfing "step back in time" which doesn't beat you up too badly… Himalayas and Cardinal alone are worth the price of admission… I absolutely love this course… Relies entirely on the history. History aside, it remains enjoyable and very playable… Pick of the holes was 15, a blind narrow tee shot and a blind approach to a green that runs away from you. 17 is the most bizarre hole I have ever played, confusing in some ways… There are blind shots, rolling fairways, steeply banked greens, dunes, gigantic bunkers straight in your path, and hidden pot bunkers that are almost impossible to get out of – everything that golf was… Loved every aspect, risk and reward shots and even the blind tee shot at the 5th… A pure, raw, testing and pensive round of golf… Come here with a different attitude, and accept it for what it is, a trip into the history of golf… It's a winner!

Prestwick is a traditional monument, an authentic affair with a layout of holes that snake to and fro through rugged dunes and rippled fairways. There are numerous blind holes and cavernous sleepered bunkers with wooden steps to take you down to the bottom. The greens are notoriously firm and fast – some are hidden in hollows whilst others are perched on raised plateaus. The majority are quite small and all of them have wicked borrows to negotiate.

One of Prestwick's great strengths is the quality and variety of the holes. The 1st is one of the most intimidating holes in golf, a par 4 called "Railway". The railway tracks run all the way down the right-hand side of the hole, waiting to gobble up a right-hander's slice. The 3rd is a short par five (SI 1) called "Cardinal" and is famous for its deep, deep bunker, propped up by railway sleepers. The 5th is a blind par 3 called "Himalayas" – your tee shot must carry over a huge sand dune.

There are so many great things to say about Prestwick. The best thing to do is to play the course and judge it yourself.

David Fleming – Club Professional writes:

Prestwick is a relaxed and friendly golf club that enjoys hosting golfers who come from around the world to enjoy this testing and traditional links. The club was founded in 1851 and Old Tom Morris designed the course. Old Tom was also the club's first "Keeper of the Green, Ball and Club Maker". Prestwick was the birthplace of the Open Golf Championship – first staged in 1860 – and has hosted the championship 24 times in all. The club has also staged the British Amateur Championship on a number of occasions.

Sand, heather, seaside bent grasses, cavernous bunkers, sloping fairways, the menacing Pow Burn, fast, true and undulating greens, delightful views of the Island of Arran and the wind, sometimes a zephyr, sometimes half a gale, prevailing mostly from the southwest. All these ingredients combine to make Prestwick a fantastic golfing challenge and a course that simply should not be missed.

Machrihanish

MACHRIHANISH GOLF CLUB
Machrihanish, Campbeltown, Argyll, PA28 6PT, Scotland
Telephone: +44 (0) 1586 810213
Website: www.machgolf.com
Architect: Old Tom Morris
Visitors: Welcome – no restrictions

Average Reviewers' Score:

Reviewers' Comments

Machrihanish is as beautiful and as enjoyable as either Turnberry or Dornoch… It is without doubt my number one golfing pleasure… You get a feeling of stepping back in time to when golf was a simple, uncomplicated game… Worth savouring, matched by only a few courses in the world for quality of golf, setting, experience and "pleasurable excitement"… Each drive seemed more demanding than the one before (and remember the first!)… Opening hole is great, but the real beauty of the links lies between holes 3 and 16… 8 is one of the best par 4s you will find anywhere, and number 10 one of the best par 5s in the country… Course never plays the same way, the weather constantly changes and therefore strategy is key… Views are staggering and I doubt that there is anywhere else in Scotland to match the vistas across to Islay, Jura & Gigha… Playing experience is worth every minute of the full day needed to savour its delights… Well worth a visit, you will not be disappointed.

Peter Craig

The small village of Machrihanish is situated on the western side of the remote Kintyre Peninsula; this is where the sky is big, the sunsets are dramatic and the air has been warmed by the Gulf Stream. Nearby Campbeltown was once the whisky capital of the world, but today only the Springbank distillery remains in full operation.

Machrihanish Golf Club must be one of the most natural, romantic and most enjoyable places to play golf in the whole of the British Isles. It's not long, grand or a championship course, but it is sheer fun. It's got an outstanding front nine and a thrilling start. The greens are firm, fast, true and are positioned in the most varied of locations. Some are sunk in punchbowls whilst others are on a raised plateau or flattened dune tops. There are blind tee shots, fabulous sea views, undulating rippling fairways and exciting rugged dunes. You have to make an extra special effort to get to Machrihanish, but it is worth it. The welcome is extraordinarily friendly and the golf is extraordinary.

Ken Campbell – PGA Golf Professional writes:

Machrihanish has become well known in the last few years mainly because of its exceptional first hole which requires the opening shot to carry the Atlantic. It's a tough start, particularly into a breeze.

The course is set in wonderful dunes a few miles west of Campbeltown in Argyll and its relative inaccessibility has saved it from becoming more commercialised.
It is a joy to play and, most of the time, very quiet, allowing the visitor to relish the ups and downs of the fairways and the tussle with undulating greens. There are also arresting views across to the islands of Jura and Islay which provide a delightful backdrop on an idyllic summer's day with the firm Machrihanish turf underfoot, the majesty of the dunes and wheeling seabirds providing the only sound.

It's a varied test for the competent golfer and the layout is not just a predictable nine out and nine back. The classic links holes – apart from the 1st – are the 5th, another par four with its fairway like an elephant's graveyard, the 10th, a clever dogleg par five and the 15th, a one shotter with real difficulty if the elusive green is missed from the tee.

Peter Craig

Nairn

NAIRN GOLF CLUB
Seabank Road, Nairn, IV12 4HB, Scotland
Telephone: +44 (0) 1667 453208
Website: www.nairngolfclub.co.uk
Architect: Archie Simpson, Old Tom Morris, James Braid and Ben Sayers
Visitors: Welcome – contact in advance. Not Sat/Sun am

Average Reviewers' Score:

Reviewers' Comments

If you only have enough time to play two Highland courses, then you should chose Nairn alongside Royal Dornoch… Nairn is a truly magnificent links, maintained impeccably (best conditioned course in the Highlands)… Absolutely outstanding first class links course… The greens are like billiard table velvet and as true and as fast as you could ever wish for… Opening holes along the shore are links golf at its finest, especially the magnificent 5th… The first few holes run along the Firth, and then the course turns slightly inland to some magnificent holes… There is a brief letdown when the course incongruously moves inland for a couple of holes but the finish is testing and the whole experience exhilarating… Fantastic series of opening holes hugging the Firth. In fact, there is not a single weak hole on the course in my view… Excellent bunkering and masterful design… A classic links course… It's well worth the trip… I can't wait to get back to Nairn.

Nairn Golf Club is located on an elevated, rumpled piece of linksland on the Moray Firth coastline, close to the historic fishing port. It's one of Scotland's lesser-known gems and one of the most spectacular seaside courses in Britain, boasting sea views from every hole. If you are a right-hander and you've got a slicing problem, you could find the beach from your very first tee shot. The sea is in play on six of the first seven holes; make sure you've got an adequate supply of balls.

When the sun is low in the sky and the shadows are long, you cannot fail to appreciate the undulating, bunker-pitted moonscape that is Nairn. It's a delightful links with fast, firm but narrow fairways, a number of which are framed by gorse bushes and heather, heaping further pressure onto a nervous drive. The greens are sited in the trickiest places – some are raised and others are nestled in hollows. Most are well protected, either by bunkers or natural hazards, and all of the greens are fast and true, a Nairn trademark.

The 5th is a great 390-yard par four which requires a straight solid drive avoiding the beach on the right, leaving a short approach shot to a small, elevated green that is well protected by bunkers and a bank sloping off to the right. The 9th, named "Icehouse", is a lovely par four to close the outward nine. A tough long drive from the tee needs to avoid the whin bushes on the left and the bunkers on the right. The green is located to the right of the white cottage which is, in fact, a Salmon Bothy. Keep your eyes peeled for the Icehouse which is covered in thick grassy turf where salmon was kept on ice for up to two years.

Robin Fyfe – Professional writes:
Nairn is a delightful course nestling on the shore of the Moray Firth. After an easy opening stretch of holes alongside the firth, you will find yourself being challenged by some of the best links holes to be found anywhere. Normally in fine condition, you will find your experience of playing Nairn a real golfing treat that leaves you wanting to come back for more.

ST GEORGE'S HILL GOLF CLUB

Average Reviewers' Score:

Golf Club Road, St George's Hill, Weybridge, Surrey, KT13 0NL, England
Telephone: +44 (0) 1932 847758
Website: www.stgeorgeshillgolfclub.co.uk
Architect: Harry Colt
Visitors: Contact in advance – handicap cert require

Reviewers' Comments

The stunning clubhouse has the feel of a really comfy pair of old slippers… Course oozes charm and character and is beautifully natural… Wonderfully laid out, following the natural contours superbly… Three excellent loops of nine through undulating pine forests and heather… A great mix of fantastic driving holes, well-placed hazards and wonderfully sculpted greens – this really is a feast… All of the holes were a great test, well bunkered and with excellent greens that had many subtle and not so subtle borrows… Every hole is a challenge, with a mixture of long par 3s, some short par 4s and testing par 5s… Not a very testing golf course for the better player… Forget all that nonsense about it being a short course, all the Colt classics are… Turf is lovely and promotes a nice strike… More affordable than Sunningdale and Wentworth… Treated with warmth and friendliness by the staff and members… An all-round wonderful golfing experience… Looking forward to my next round here.

St George's Hill is the prettiest of the many heathland courses on the Surrey/ Berkshire sand belt and, in our opinion, one of the very best. In 1911, a local builder came up with an original idea to build luxury fairway-side houses and by chance, Harry Colt was the chosen architect. The course opened for play in 1913 and it is considered to be Colt's greatest work.

The most notable difference between St George's Hill and the heathland layouts in this area is the terrain. The land here sweeps and undulates like a rollercoaster and Harry Colt used these dramatic elevation changes superbly in his design.

The spectacular panorama from the front of the clubhouse, or the pavilion as it was originally called, totally whets your appetite. It is one of those views that grabs you and makes your heart pound in excited anticipation. You cannot help but want to get out onto the first tee as quickly as possible.

Amongst the grandiose setting is inherent charm and beauty. The houses beside the fairways have style and never impose and, if anything, they are complementary and add to the amazing St George's Hill experience.

Head Professional – Tony Rattue writes:
St George's Hill is a wonderfully testing layout with fir trees, sand and heather. These are beautiful things in themselves and the ingredients from which inland courses should be made. The prettiest courses are also the best and certainly one of the prettiest and the best is St George's Hill.

NORTH BERWICK GOLF CLUB

Beach Road, North Berwick, East Lothian, EH39 4BB, Scotland
Telephone: +44 (0) 1620 892135
Website: www.northberwickgolfclub.com
Architect: Unknown
Visitors: Welcome – contact in advance.

Average Reviewers' Score:

Reviewers' Comments

If I could play only one more round of golf in Scotland, I would choose North Berwick without hesitation… I can't say that North Berwick West is perfect but it's as much fun as a person could have playing golf… Somewhat bizarre, quirky links that most players fall in love with… Front 9 are good, especially the first par 3, but the second 9 are fantastic! I can't think of a better 9-hole stretch in all of Scotland… Back 9 brings you back along the ocean, with high dunes and rough dominating the scene… 13, Pit, is probably the most unique hole I've played. The green is squeezed in between the ubiquitous wall that runs through the course and a high, steeply banked dune… 14, Perfection, calls for an exhilarating shot over a hill to a green that sits down near the water. 15, the Redan hole, is justifiably famous, but 16, with a bizarre split-level green, is almost as unique… North Berwick is all about fun, fun and for those of a serious disposition… FUN!

The West Links at North Berwick is an immensely enjoyable golf course, located on the Firth of Forth with stunning sea views across to Craigleith Island and Bass Rock, a huge volcanic lump, rising up over 300 feet from the Firth of Forth.

This is a course that is extremely close to the origins of golf. It's the thirteenth oldest golf club and the second oldest course in the world still playing over its original fairways. Only the Old course at St Andrews is more senior.

There are two reasons why North Berwick is such an enjoyable course: 1) the land is raised above sea level, affording those excellent views 2) it has a superb collection of holes, a number of which have been replicated at other courses the world over.

One of the many beauties of North Berwick is that you can play the course without being punished brutally by penal rough. It's not the longest links course in the world but it's sheer fun and a unique experience to boot. You'll need to negotiate stonewalls, deep bunkers, all kinds of humps and hollows and burns. You'll need to hit blind shots and you'll need to hit shots out over the beach. Fantastic stuff.

David Huish – Head Professional writes:
To golfers everywhere North Berwick is at least a name, but the fortunate are those that know its charms at first hand. The illustrious West Links and the North Berwick Golf Club (founded in 1832) have admirably stood the test of time – along with St Andrews, Prestwick and Muirfield – it has protected and maintained its traditions and high standards as one of the most celebrated Scottish links courses.

Royal Aberdeen (Balgownie)

ROYAL ABERDEEN GOLF CLUB
Balgownie Links, Bridge of Don, Aberdeen, AB23 8AT, Scotland
Telephone: +44 (0) 1224 702571
Website: www.royalaberdeengolf.com **Architect:** Robert and
Archie Simpson, Tom Simpson, J.H Taylor, James Braid, Donald Steel
Visitors: Contact in advance – restricted at weekends

Average Reviewers' Score:

Reviewers' Comments
Simply brilliant stuff, start to finish… Better than the majority of Open Championship
rota courses… The front nine is the best 9 holes I have played and the back nine isn't
bad… Second nine is not as dramatic or visually histrionic… Tom Watson was full of
praise following the 2005 Seniors Open Championship and as a 5-time Open Champion, I
think it is fair to say that he is a good judge… Simply, this course is worth every penny of
the green fee, which is almost as steep as the vertical riveted face of the bunker front-left
of the 9th green! A must-play and if difficulty was king, would be a regular on the Open
rota… Perfect links turf and superb putting surfaces cannot be faulted… With a little
wiggle around the 8th and 9th, the course then turns to return along a plateau heading
back south towards home… Wonderful! Worth every penny… If they could cater for
40,000 a day, it would be a great Open venue… Should not be missed.

Many people believe that Royal Aberdeen has the finest first nine holes in golf. The first tee is under the clubhouse window and the fairway heads straight for the sea. The next eight holes run parallel to the shore, weaving their way through towering sand dunes. You then turn back, heading for the clubhouse. The back nine holes play on higher ground and provide stunning North Sea views.

While the front nine holes are undoubtedly excellent, the back nine holes are probably harder. They are more exposed to the elements, and consequently, bear the full brunt of the wind. The par threes are also first class, as is the finishing hole, a brutal par four, in excess of 400 yards. A good tee shot will finish in a hollow in the fairway, leaving a long second shot across a swale to an elevated green perched in front of the clubhouse.

This is an excellent traditional links course, but make sure you haven't spent too much time looking for your ball in the rough. The five-minute rule was made here back in 1783.

Ronnie MacAskill – Director of Golf writes:
Robert and Archie Simpson designed the course; James Braid, J. H. Taylor and most recently Donald Steel undertook later changes. The course runs essentially out and back along the North Sea shore. The outward nine runs through some wonderful dune formations and the inward nine on a plateau. The outward nine at Royal Aberdeen has long been acknowledged as one of the finest in the world. A traditional old Scottish links, well bunkered with undulating fairways.

An excellent balance of holes, strong par 4s, tricky par 3s with the 8th protected by 10 bunkers (our signature hole) and classic par 5s.

The ever-changing wind, small greens and a very challenging finish make Royal Aberdeen a test for every level of golfer.

Aidan Bradley

SAUNTON GOLF CLUB
Braunton, North Devon, EX33 1LG, England
Telephone: +44 (0) 1271 812436
Website: www.sauntongolf.co.uk
Architect: Herbert Fowler
Visitors: Book in advance – handicap certificate required

Average Reviewers' Score:

Reviewers' Comments

Far and away the best course we played while staying the west of England… Standing at the first tee is quite an experience… Classic links extend all around you as you reach for the driver… Simply magnificent golf… A course with so much potential – the 18 holes are near perfect… Hard fast fairways and greens, wispy long rough and great routing… Length is not the problem but trouble lurks just off every fairway… Found the course not overlong from the white markers – only the 1st, 4th and 14th (toughest hole) made us struggle but there is relief in the aptly named 5th 'Tiddler'… Layout/set-up is good and you do seem to be 'on your own hole' a lot of the time… Selection of par 3s, 4s and a couple of 5s are great… Really enjoyed ourselves and our only regret was not having the time or stamina for the West course… If Saunton was located in East Lothian, it would perhaps be considered to be one of the greatest courses on the planet.

Alex Sherratt

Saunton is located on the beautiful unspoilt North Devon coast. On the edge of Bideford Bay and the estuary of the River Taw, lie the Braunton Burrows. Unesco has designated the sand dunes at Braunton Burrows of international importance and it is the first site in the UK to become a biosphere reserve.

The East course, laid out in 1897, runs through a small part of this amazing expanse of sand dunes. Herbert Fowler added a bit of redesign magic in 1919 and very little has changed since. Fowler took full advantage of the natural terrain, routing the holes through the dunes with skill. Saunton is his finest seaside creation and Harry Vardon loved it, saying: "I would like to retire to Saunton and do nothing but play golf for pleasure."

It's a tough golf course. The East has eight par fours over 400 yards long and only two par fives. Scoring well is very difficult, even more so now that the 2nd hole – once a short par five – has been lengthened to almost 530 yards. There are two excellent short par threes, which demand accuracy, and there's the tough 207-yard 17th hole, which often needs a decent crack with a wood.

Albert MacKenzie – Club Professional writes:
Saunton East is a truly wonderful links venue, set in traditional links terrain, and is widely acclaimed as the finest seaside course never to have hosted The Open. The golf course bares its teeth early on with the opening 4 holes totalling over one mile in length! By the time you reach the 5th tee it often seems like you've completed a marathon, never mind a mile.

The Par 3s, 5 and 13, are both less than 150 yards in length, but will test the best with their undulating features. Henry Longhurst had the 16th hole in his "Best 18" on the British Isles and it easy to see why. The East course will reward a good driver of the ball and the design of the course will allow for frequent use of this club should you so wish. This is simply links golf at its finest and should not be missed.

Alex Sherratt

ST ENODOC GOLF CLUB
Rock, Wadebridge, Cornwall, PL27 6LD, England
Telephone: +44 (0) 1208 862200
Website: www.st-enodoc.co.uk
Architect: James Braid
Visitors: Contact in advance – handicap certificate required

Average Reviewers' Score:

Reviewers' Comments

Wherever you live, it's worth the trip to Cornwall just to play St Enodoc... I can recall every hole – a sign of a truly memorable golf course... Amazing views from virtually every hole as well as an excellent test of golf (particularly in the wind)... Good value for money and full of excitement with fairways that look like rippled waves... The rollercoaster of 'sporty' holes relieved me of my thoughts of having mastered this game. I blame the scenery for distracting me at almost every tee box, fairway and green... Played badly and loved every minute of it! Take a moment to visit the church, if possible. Visit the grave of Betjeman, recite the famous poem and pray for a birdie or two, to restore your golfing soul... One of the best finishes in links golf... It's a dream come true for anyone who enjoys golf and holds a current handicap certificate... Experience is magical, almost trance-like... Truly a privilege to have played this jewel... St Enodoc is one of my personal favourite courses.

St Enodoc Golf Club is located at the royal sailing town of Rock, the links overlooking the Camel Estuary and the picturesque harbour of Padstow beyond. The Church course at St Enodoc takes its name from the tiny 13th century place of worship that stands to the right of the 10th green. In the middle of the 19th century, a fierce storm completely covered the church in sand and it was eventually extricated in 1863.

It's a quixotic links, set amidst towering sand dunes clad with tufts of wild sea grasses. The fairways undulate and ripple just as if the sea had ebbed only moments ago. We have to own up – this is one of our favourite links courses because the terrain is entirely natural. The dunes are so pronounced that you cannot help but feel humbled, the holes are varied and charming and, finally, so much of the experience is memorable.

There are many great holes, but the 6th is a bit of a collector's item, a hole of absolute uniqueness, a blind drive followed by a blind mid iron second shot which must carry over a confrontational sand dune called "Himalayas". This stands some 100 yards out, guarding the hidden green. Let's be honest, this is an enormous dune, worthy of its name, rising up over 75 feet high. Make sure you get your club selection right and that you strike the ball cleanly!

If your ball happens to come to rest in the churchyard after a wayward shot, keep an eye out for John Betjeman's headstone. The Poet Laureate lies buried amidst his favourite seaside course. After a rare birdie on the 13th, he penned his famous poem "Seaside Golf".

James W. Finegan writes:
I suspect that if a genie were to appear before me at this moment with an offer to transport me magically to any course in the world, I just might choose this nonpareil on the wild north coast of Cornwall.

CARNE GOLF LINKS
Carne, Belmullet, Co. Mayo, Ireland
Telephone: + 353 (0)97 82292
Website: www.carnegolflinks.com
Architect: Eddie Hackett
Visitors: Welcome – contact in advance

Average Reviewers' Score:

Reviewers' Comments

Can I give Carne one hundred wee golf balls on your rating system? So much fun that it's not even funny... Exhilarating and unpretentious... Never enjoyed a round of golf so much in my life... Better than most Open Championship venues... Golfing nirvana... Fusion of amazing Irish landscape and crafty design... Round builds hole after hole with each becoming harder and more spectacular... I believe the secret to Mr Hackett's design is purely what he hasn't done... Has evolved from the land in the way that great links courses should... If there are 18 better holes of links golf in the world, they will have to be unbelievable... You have no idea what the next tee holds for you – other than yet another enormous smile... If you've never been – then go – it is truly something more than just a 'game of golf'! If I won the lottery I would buy a life membership, a helicopter and spend every weekend playing here... Journey is worth the effort and the welcome and hospitality difficult to beat.

The Carne Golf Links at Belmullet is the late Eddie Hackett's swansong and many reckon it's his finest design. The course sits in splendid isolation on the Atlantic edge of County Mayo. It lies on a peninsula, amidst gigantic dunes with far-reaching views across the bay to the Atlantic islands of Inis Gloire and Inis Geidhewild. And it's absolutely charming.

Carne is wild, and natural. It's difficult to believe that the course only opened for play in the mid 1990s. It feels as though it's been here forever. Many of the greens and tees are sited naturally and, for such a modern course, very little earth-moving was required during the construction. From spring to late autumn, the course is alive with harebells, sea holly and wild thyme.

If you haven't heard of Carne, it could be your golf course find of the century. You'll certainly remember the lunar landscape and the towering sand dunes. A trip to Ireland's beautiful west coast would not be complete without playing one of the world's most naturally beautiful links courses.

Eamon Mangan – Director and Founder Member

Even though Carne only opened in 1995, it appears as if it has been there for centuries. The topography of the links-land at Carne is amazing. Huge elevation changes and fairways along valleys that wind through towering dunes and the spectacular views of Broadhaven Bay and the wild Atlantic Ocean will take your breath away.

When the course architect, the late Eddie Hackett, first walked the lands at Carne, he said: "We must keep what the good Lord has given us here... I will put in greens and tees, but the rest is already here, provided and sculptured by the elements over time." One golf journalist, after playing Carne, wrote: "It is a no-holds-barred celebration of the joy of golf, the test and the surprise and the sport and the sheer delight of the game, in a setting of colossal sandhills." The result of Eddie's work is now rewarded, as Carne has taken its rightful place among the great links courses in the world.

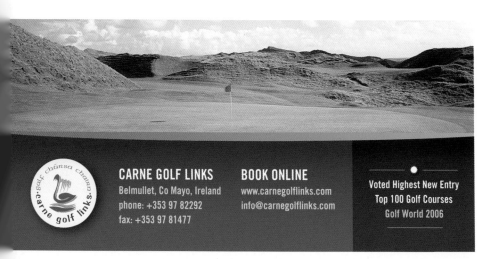

CARNE GOLF LINKS
Belmullet, Co Mayo, Ireland
phone: +353 97 82292
fax: +353 97 81477

BOOK ONLINE
www.carnegolflinks.com
info@carnegolflinks.com

Voted Highest New Entry
Top 100 Golf Courses
Golf World 2006

Hillside

HILLSIDE GOLF CLUB
Hastings Road, Hillside, Southport, Merseyside, PR8 2LU, England
Telephone: +44 (0) 1704 567169
Website: www.hillside-golfclub.co.uk
Architect: Fred Hawtree, Donald Steel
Visitors: Contact in advance – not weekends

Average Reviewers' Score:

Reviewers' Comments
What a course! Why is this course not rated higher as it deserves to be right up there amongst the very top rated tracks? I can only agree with all the reviews before that Hillside is a great course and for less than half the money of Royal Birkdale it is great value... Absolutely FANTASTIC golf course... If you are in Southport and only get the opportunity to play one course then play Hillside... Loved every moment of my four hours on the course...The back 9 is possibly the very best in England... And then the back nine – what a treat! Elevated tees abound with immaculate sleepered stepping and closely mown grass banks – very classy... Putting surfaces have grass replaced with green velvet – only kidding, but it seemed that way, they were so good! The 10th is described as possibly the best par three in GB&I – easy to see why... Lovely welcoming members – cannot wait to go back and experience this course again... Great experience indeed... This is a future Open Course in waiting... Golf heaven without doubt.

Kevin Murray

There are eight top-notch seaside courses between St Annes and Liverpool and many people believe that this is the best stretch of linksland in the British Isles. It is certainly England's links golfing Mecca.

Hillside is an underrated gem, separated only by a footpath, but hiding in the shadow of its noble next-door neighbour, Royal Birkdale. The railway line separates Hillside from Southport and Ainsdale, another superb but relatively unknown links.

Today's layout is very different to the original Hillside that was founded in 1911. The club acquired some new land in the 1960s and Fred Hawtree extensively remodelled the course, making major changes to the back nine. The front nine has always been highly regarded and plays over relatively flat ground, but it's the homeward nine that is really special and is frequently bracketed alongside Ballybunion because the holes ripple and undulate through the giant dunes.

Hillside has many strong and individual holes but the 11th has everything going for it. A reachable par five of just over 500 yards that doglegs left, the elevated tee provides a panoramic view of the hole in play and many other holes too, not only at Hillside but also at Royal Birkdale and Southport & Ainsdale.

Brian Seddon – PGA Professional writes:
Although Hillside is Royal Birkdale's near neighbour, it is never in its shadow and many would rank both courses equally. Hillside is set amongst glorious sandhills and also several holes are tree-lined.

The back nine were routed through huge sand dunes and these holes combine to provide a thrilling and dramatic closing sequence which is regarded by many as one of golf's best inward stretches.

Hillside is not only a regular Open Qualifying course but the club also played host to the PGA Championship in 1982, which was Tony Jacklin's last notable tour victory.

Kevin Murray

OLD HEAD GOLF LINKS
Kinsale, Co. Cork, Ireland
Telephone: +353 (0) 21 477 8444
Website: www.oldhead.com
Architect: Joe Carr and Ron Kirby
Visitors: Book in advance – closed during winter

Average Reviewers' Score:

Reviewers' Comments
Simply jaw-dropping… Old Head is fun, scary, exciting and a place that is totally unforgettable… I have never been so scared over so many shots… Yes I know it's not a traditional links and it's slightly more expensive than anywhere else in the region, but this is the most spectacular golfing experience you'll probably ever have and all I have to say is words cannot do it justice and seeing is believing… Starts with a straightforward 1st hole to get you in the groove… I will never forget the feeling of walking from the 1st green and approaching the 2nd tee… Many holes have a tee and a green and nature does the rest… As with any course, some holes are stronger than others but the 12th is truly remarkable… Give yourself a treat… Just do it and forget the cost… Sumptuous clubhouse and levels of service uncommon in Ireland… This is a once-in-a-lifetime experience that everyone should enjoy… Pure exhilaration.

Laid out on a narrow headland, jutting out for two miles into the Atlantic Ocean, Old Head has to be one of the world's most exhilarating sites upon which golf is played. You feel as though you are on the edge of the world and if you suffer from vertigo, some of the tees might present a problem. Three hundred feet up, looking over the edge of the cliff, you will notice seagulls gliding below you. Atlantic waves crash onto the rocks, booming and echoing as they smash into the cave tunnels. It certainly takes your breath away.

Take some extra golf balls; you may well lose a few unless you are really on top of your game. There is little margin for error along the edges of the holes bordering the cliff-tops. The signs should be adhered to; they warn you off looking for balls for obvious reasons! Take note of the marker posts, or should we say "Stones of Accord" (the club's logo) – they give you the right line for your tee shot.

There are many memorable holes at Old Head but our favourite is the do-or-die par five 12th – it's one of the most outrageous holes in golf – whatever you do with your tee shot, don't bite-off more than you can chew.

Keith Baxter writes:
I've been fortunate to play Old Head on numerous occasions since it opened in 1997 and for once the marketing hype does not do it justice. "The most spectacular golf course on earth... Unrivalled in terms of the magnificent beauty and setting of the site... The promontory is almost an island with numerous caves running beneath your feet as you play the course." These words and more are true and nothing can prepare you for the magnificence of the 2nd hole and the thrill of the tee shot on the 12th raises goosebumps. This may not be the most architecturally proficient golf course on the Emerald Isle but the adrenaline-pumping site will blow the socks off most mortals.

WESTERN GAILES GOLF CLUB
Gailes, Irvine, Ayrshire, KA11 5AE, Scotland
Telephone: +44 (0) 1294 311649
Website: www.westerngailes.com
Architect: Willie Park, Fred Hawtree
Visitors: Welcome Mon, Wed & Fri – contact in advance

Average Reviewers' Score:

Reviewers' Comments

Western Gailes is one of the hidden gems of Scottish golf... Great links squashed between the railway and the sea... Understated gem of the Ayrshire coast... Doesn't have the pedigree of Turnberry, Troon or Prestwick, but in many ways Western is the best all-round course of the bunch... There are no unfair or obvious designer hallmarks... A sense of quiet and unassuming confidence is all around the place and there's nothing showy, just a good honest links course with a fine collection of holes and an especially strong set of par threes... 7 is a great par three, hard against the coastline with the green nestled between high banks of rough... Most of the time the wind is either dead with or against you... Nine consecutive holes into the wind become a little tedious! Holes are all interesting and challenging... Will appeal to the connoisseurs... Clubhouse is imposing but welcoming and the staff and members are really friendly... Make sure it's at the top of your list of courses to play.

Western Gailes Golf Club is wedged between Irvine Bay and the railway tracks on one of Ayrshire's narrowest strips of links land. Western and its next-door neighbour, Glasgow Gailes, are the northernmost of the exceptional links courses located on this prodigious stretch of Ayrshire coastline.

It's an unusual layout in that the clubhouse is more or less centrally located. The first four holes head north, parallel to the railway tracks. The next nine holes head straight back along the coastline in a southerly direction, passing the clubhouse along the way, and then the closing five holes head northwards, back towards the clubhouse and once more along the railway line.

Whilst the layout, as we have already mentioned, is unusual but ostensibly nine out and nine back, the holes are wonderfully varied. The fairways undulate gently, interrupted occasionally by three meandering burns that dissect this thin strip of land. The greens sites are cleverly located in naturally folded ground; burns protect some whilst others, like the 6th, are in hollows guarded by sand dunes. All the greens are fast, firm and subtly contoured. The 14th hole, a wonderful par five which often plays downwind, provides a huge temptation for big hitters, but numerous bunkers lie in wait.

Be prepared for a westerly wind that can be undeniably ferocious and cunning as it switches direction from southwesterly to northwesterly. On occasions it can be soul-destroying. Western Gailes is a suitably fitting name for this golf course.

James W. Finegan writes:
The holes are laid out on a long, narrow strip of land between – you will have already guessed it – the sea and the railway line. You can slice into both. There are dunes and heather and gorse, and long, spiky marram grass. On terrain that offers very little in the way of elevation changes, there are gently raised tees and greens in dune-framed dells and on exposed plateaux. On seven holes burns make us think twice… By careful count, there are 100 bunkers, some of them deep pots where a stroke is irretrievably lost.

Silloth on Solway

SILLOTH ON SOLWAY GOLF CLUB

Average Reviewers' Score:

The Club House, Silloth on Solway, Cumbria, CA7 4BL, England
Telephone: +44 (0) 16973 31304
Website: www.sillothgolfclub.co.uk
Architect: Davy Grant, Willie Park Jnr
Visitors: Contact in advance

Reviewers' Comments

It's the best course I have ever played... Lovely scenic views over the Solway... A wonderful links course... Starts out with a drive over a sand dune with the green set below... A good, old fashioned out and back layout with a real wild, untamed feel to the terrain – it's very natural and nothing is tricked up here... Holes have a great variety of twists and turns, and every hole turns out to be much more of a test than you would think by looking at the card... Blind carries and the vagaries of the links bounce test the players resolve... Short par three 9th is one of the great short par threes in the world... You will not get better value anywhere in the UK for a Top 50 course... If I had to play my last ever round of golf you'd find me on the 1st tee at Silloth on Solway... It really is a remote jewel that shines brightly in the northwest corner of England... Golf as it should be.

Silloth on Solway Golf Club was founded in 1892, with the help of Railway Company money. Davy Grant and Willie Park Jnr. originally designed it and it is a club famous for its affiliation with ladies' golf. Silloth has parliamentary connections too. Viscount Willie Whitelaw was the Club President until his death in 1999.

You have to make an extra special effort to get to Silloth because it is located in one of the most remote and isolated places in England, at the mouth of the Solway Firth. But the winding road trip is truly worthwhile.

With heather and gorse adding brilliant splashes of seasonal colour, Silloth is a cracking links golf course. When the wind blows, it's unlikely that you will play to your handicap. Even on a calm day, you'll find it tough. "It is also the home of the winds," wrote Darwin, "when I was there the wind did not blow really hard, but hard enough to make a fool of me." Finding the tight greens is no mean feat either, and when you do, they are tough to read with their subtle borrows.

It's well worth the time (and the money) to get to Silloth and once you get there, you won't want to leave. You are at one of the best value golf courses in the whole of the British Isles.

Jonathan Graham – Head Professional writes:

Silloth is an enchanting course and the very epitome of the phrase "hidden gem".

Each hole has its own charm and unique feel and will test all your skills especially your short game. While obviously an advantage, length is not terribly important at Silloth; there is a premium on accuracy. Miss the fairways and you will be punished and if you manage to find the fairway chances are you won't have a very flat lie to cope with.

The signature hole is the 13th, which at 518 yards is not a long par five by modern standards. But it is a wonderfully testing hole, a real risk or reward decision. And when you eventually reach the green, you are greeted by stunning views across the Solway Firth and Lake District.

im McCann

DOONBEG GOLF CLUB
Doonbeg, Co. Clare, Ireland
Telephone: +353 (0) 659 055 246
Website: www.doonbeggolfclub.com
Architect: Greg Norman
Visitors: Welcome, with restrictions, contact in advance

Average Reviewers' Score:

Reviewers' Comments

I wondered whether Doonbeg would be a disappointment "in the flesh". It was not; it's a terrific golf course. Pure links with tight lies, sand everywhere, the smell of the sea and some holes played almost in the sea... While it lies among the sand dunes and occupies a spectacular setting, the course fails to live up to its billing... Doonbeg is pure G. Standing on the 1st tee must be one of the most attractive opening scenes in golf... Course has a lot of excellent holes, some truly great holes and unique features e.g. 12th green with a bunker in the middle, incredible greens and one disappointing hole... 14th is fine for the single digit handicapper to take it on with vengeance, but those of us mid teens 'cappers better have at least a sleeve ready for this one, along with a good sense of humour... Stunning... Whole experience was fantastic... A wonderful mix of US hospitality and Irish charm... I can't wait to go back again... Greg has done a magnificent job.

Steve Uzzell - Doonbeg Glf Club

You'll find Doonbeg 40 minutes or so due west of Shannon airport. Just keep going until you reach the Atlantic. You can't miss the golf course — just look out for the mountainous dunes and keep your eyes peeled and somewhere around these spectacular 100ft high sandhills, you might get a glimpse of the Great White Shark. Because this is the course that Greg Norman built - his one and only British/Irish architectural ensemble.

Apparently Norman made 23 visits to this amazing piece of links-land, which curves and tumbles for a mile and a half around the crescent-shaped Doughmore Bay. Norman's design is totally in tune with nature – 14 greens and 12 fairways were simply mown – not much earth moved for Greg here at Doonbeg. The look and feel of the layout is old-fashioned and the routing follows an out-and-back style, synonymous with traditional links architecture.

The layout is unusual in that it has a combination of five par threes and five par fives – the par 72 course measures 6,885 yards from the back tees. The signature hole is probably the 14th, a par three and one of the most sensational short holes in Ireland, although there are many memorable holes on this remarkable course. The 14th measures a mere 111 yards, but hitting the green is easier said than done because there are numerous distractions... the Atlantic stretches out beyond the green and the wind will dictate your club selection. Expect to take anything from a sand wedge to a 3 iron and hope for the best.

Greg Norman writes:
I have designed the course around the 15th hole, a magnificent par four of 440 yards to a funnel-shaped green surrounded by the highest dunes on the course. Landing a ball on the front edge of the 150-foot-long green, and wondering if it will stop before running off the far end (into perdition), is far more of a challenge to me than the target golf of hitting behind the flagstick from 187 yards and spinning it back six inches.

Formby

FORMBY GOLF CLUB
Golf Road, Formby, Merseyside, L37 1LQ, England
Telephone: +44 (0) 1704 872164
Website: www.formbygolfclub.co.uk
Architect: Willie Park, James Braid, Hawtree and Taylor, Donald Steel
Visitors: Contact in advance

Average Reviewers' Score:

Reviewers' Comments

The strength of Formby is the layout. Every hole is different... Fantastic course and you wouldn't expect to find trees on that stretch of the coast... The fir tree emblem on ball markers, hole flags and such-like tells you all you need to know about Formby – it is dominated by trees of the pine variety which are used to good effect throughout the course... A superb course and what a deal in early November... Good condition with the greens true and quick... The best greens we played on too... Greens were such that your putting improved because their quality and pace demanded full concentration... Marvellous conditioning and heavenly hole routing in an anti-clockwise circle... Was a great challenge with well-placed bunkers... Much of a heathland feel to it... A real beast from the back tees... Holes 7 to 9 were particularly strong, with hole 7 the pick of the trio... Formby was a very fine place to play and a double bill of golf here and at Hillside would be a great day out.

Formby is a unique course as the holes are routed in a huge anti-clockwise circle around the Formby Ladies' Club which sits slap bang in the middle of the men's course. The first three holes follow the railway line, the 4th turns and heads out towards the Irish Sea and at the turn, we meander back home, zigzagging up and down along the way.

The club has hosted a number of important amateur events over the years and played host to the 2004 Curtis Cup. After an exciting finish, the United States successfully retained the trophy, winning 10-8. The Amateur Championship was played here on three occasions; José Maria Olazábal emerged as the 1984 winner.

Play Formby when you have been sufficiently beaten up by the other windy links courses around Liverpool and Southport, but don't be fooled into thinking that this course is easy. It certainly is not. Bunkering is strategic, the undulating fairways are very much links-like, the rough is strewn with heather and the pines provide an element of park-like protection from the wind. Formby will suit both links lovers and the player who prefers the softness of inland golf; both these camps will arrive contentedly at the 19th watering hole.

Gary H. Butler – Head Professional writes:
Formby is a magnificent golf links, set quite uniquely amidst a profusion of pine trees, and it's the centrepiece in the string of world-class golf courses that stretch between Southport and Liverpool.

There are so many great golf holes that it is difficult to single any out, but the par five 8th is one of my favourites, requiring careful thought and a strategy. If you can hit it long and straight, this hole may yield a birdie. If you are offline, you'll be in the trees and struggling for par. The 12th is a beautiful hole visually but the little par three 16th can be a card-wrecker. With three deep pot bunkers and a green that slopes away from you, a par here is always a good score.

Kevin Murray

Swinley Forest

SWINLEY FOREST GOLF CLUB
Coronation Road, Ascot, Berkshire, SL5 9LE, England
Telephone: +44 (0) 1344 874979
Website: None
Architect: Harry Colt
Visitors: By invitation only

Average Reviewers' Score:

Reviewers' Comments

This is one of those revered, must-play courses that I was dying to play simply because of its reputation and exclusivity… Having played many of the best heathland courses, I can say that this is one of them… We played a two ball in just over three hours. It was bliss… Despite the seemingly short nature of the course – apart from the two par 5s and two of the par 4s – the rest of the par 4s were all very solid, and the par 3s were mostly long and tricky… Par 3s are the highlight, all requiring a good iron shot… 5th was my favourite hole – a gently half-moon dogleg from a lovely raised tee with the only small lake on the course two thirds of the way down on the right… Very springy sandy soil and terrain which is more undulating than you would expect… A treat that should not be missed if you are given the opportunity… Old-school clubhouse adds the to the enjoyment… If you can get an invitation, you have to play it.

Andy Taylor

Swinley Forest is an absolutely charming golf course on the famous Surrey/ Berkshire sand belt, but it's a club that is frozen in time, exclusive, unusual and totally eccentric. In fact, you would be hard pressed to describe it as a conventional golf club: there is no captain and despite being in existence for nearly 100 years, no history, except in its members' heads. Only recently have scorecards been printed, holes allocated par figures, and competitions introduced for Swinley's distinguished gentlemen members.

Harry Colt designed the layout and the course opened for play in 1909, reputedly Colt's favourite and finest design. One of the many delights of Swinley is the ambience and the fact that it's unpretentious. It has none of the glamour of its near neighbours Sunningdale and Wentworth, but what Swinley Forest does have is bags of style.

We will make no bones about it – Swinley is a beautiful course. The short, one-shot holes are simply outstanding. The site/position of the greens sets Swinley apart from many other courses. Although the yardage is only a little over 6,000 yards, the par of 68 makes it a real challenge.

If you are lucky enough to play in late spring, look out for the rhododendrons (actually you can't miss them), they are simply breathtaking. Combine this with swathes of purple heather and lovely springy fairways winding their way through mature pines and this really is a special place. Drop a letter in the post to the secretary by way of introduction, or maybe telephone him. Who knows, he might let you play this amazing private members' course.

James W. Finegan writes:
Swinley is very short – 6,062 yards. Par is 69 in this interesting mix of eleven two-shotters, five par threes, and two par fives. Fairways are broad, forced carries are not cruel and bunkering inclines to be light. Heather, however, seems to be everywhere that grass is not.

Andy Taylor

ROYAL WEST NORFOLK GOLF CLUB
Brancaster, Norfolk, PE31 8AX, England
Telephone: +44 (0) 1485 210223
Website: None
Architect: Holcombe Ingleby
Visitors: Contact in advance – restricted at weekends

Average Reviewers' Score:

Reviewers' Comments

Without a doubt, the best golf course in the British Isles... Wonderful experience - I felt as if I had gone back in time... A course of abundant character and majesty but despair, therefore, that it remains in constant danger of tidal destruction... Even a bad round is made enjoyable by the wonderful views... Beautiful, unpredictable, tough and friendly, and the added charm of numerous well behaved Black Labradors and Springer Spaniels accompanying many of the golfers... One will have to search hard to find a hole more intelligently designed than the 3rd or more picturesque than the 8th and 9th... Brancaster is a challenge to both your physical and mental game – it's a golfing game of chess, and you are constantly under fear of "checkmate" from the deep, sleeper-faced bunkers, the hard and long rough, the wind and water, delightful! The epitome of golfing tradition... Time-warp golf... This course is unique within the British Isles... The soul of this course is hard to define but easy to feel... Magnificent.

Royal West Norfolk Golf Club is a classic and nothing much has changed here for 100 years. Squeezed beautifully between Brancaster Bay and the salt marshes, it truly is a peaceful golf links, except when the wind blows and boy, is the wind bracing here!

Check the tide times before you plan your trip. The course plays on a narrow strip of links-land which gets cut off at high tide, turning it into an island. If you are lucky enough to play the course during high tide, you are in for a real treat; the downside is that you will need plenty of golf balls.

Out on the course, you feel delightfully isolated; often all you can hear are the seductive sounds of the wind, the seagulls, the clinking of stays and the flapping of boat sails. Essentially, the course is a traditional out and back links; huge sleeper-faced bunkers, fast greens and that beautiful links turf. A magical place to play golf.

Simon Rayner – PGA Professional writes:
Royal West Norfolk Golf Club is discreetly situated on the North Norfolk coast, at the end of a tidal road. The course is surrounded by land preserved by The National Trust, including a beautiful sandy beach. The driving range is positioned on a Site of Special Scientific Interest (SSSI) as it's home to thousands of migrating birds and the wildlife that frequents the salt marshes.

The course moves away from the clubhouse and is played entirely on a sand spit, which stretches from Brancaster to Brancaster Staithe Harbour. It's pretty much nine holes out and nine holes back with traditional tight lies on the fairways, medium-sized greens and some cavernous sleepered bunkers. The addition of tidal flooding onto parts of the course make it a true test of golf whilst adding to the delight of this golfing experience.

Simon Rayner

SUNNINGDALE GOLF CLUB
Ridgemount Road, Sunningdale, Berkshire, SL5 9RR, England
Telephone: +44 (0) 1344 621681
Website: www.sunningdale-golfclub.co.uk
Architect: Harry Colt
Visitors: Contact in advance - Not Fri, Sat, Sun or public holidays

Average Reviewers' Score:

Reviewers' Comments
The New course is perhaps the most underrated layout in the country and it does not get the accolades it deserves... I've played here on many occasions and a word about the club itself, stunning... Sunningdale really has style and it doesn't really matter whether you play the Old or the New, they are both first class courses... The New is not that new really, dating back to the 1920s, but its routing is exemplary and bunker placement both cunning and cruel... It's more challenging and plays on higher ground... This is a driver's course and if you get it away well off the tee, the chances are you'll score well... The New is now a tremendous test of golf... It's a real driver's course... Numerous doglegs make the New a challenge and it helps if you can shape the ball in both directions... It's a strategic course... Either way, both Old and New are both superb, but for me, the New just has the edge... Sunningdale is a club anyone would be proud to be a member of... The best 36-hole experience, bar none.

Andy Taylor

Taken together, the New and Old courses at Sunningdale represent the finest 36 holes of golf in the whole of the British Isles. The same architect who made modifications to Sunningdale's Old course, Harry Colt, designed the New course, which opened for play in 1923 to meet the ever-increasing demand for golf.

This is a superb driving course for it is more open than the Old; the trees do not encroach quite so much. Having said this, the New demands long carries from its elevated tees over heathery terrain to narrow fairways. The club has been following a programme of regeneration that has involved the felling of a number of trees, thereby allowing the heather to return. In addition, this has cleared the way for long lost views to reappear across to Chobham Common in the south.

Many people will come to Sunningdale hell-bent on playing the Old course, but if it's a real athletic challenge you are after, you will get severely tested on the rugged 6,700-yard par 70 New, a tougher, more rounded test of golf than the Old. So far, nobody has yet managed to better Jack Nicklaus's course record of 67, which is a testament to the technical test that the New course throws up.

Keith Maxwell – Head Professional writes:
Sunningdale's Old and New courses sit side by side and provide two very different tests of golf.

The New is perhaps a more challenging test and, unlike the Old, starts as it means to go on with a long uphill par four which is followed by a par three, short par four and the 4th – a long testing par four. From this point onwards the course does not let up until perhaps the 18th – par five – finish.

The New has always been much more exposed to the elements and defends itself with five great par threes. This is a great example of Harry Colt's architecture. As a result of these two great courses, Sunningdale has always been a place that demands and rewards good golf.

K Club (Palmer)

THE K CLUB
Straffan, Co. Kildare, Ireland
Telephone: +353 (0) 1601 7200
Website: www.kclub.com
Architect: Arnold Palmer
Visitors: Contact in advance

Average Reviewers' Score:

Reviewers' Comments

The K Club is a very special place and you can tell as soon as you approach the estate, the grounds are just unbelievable... It's an impressive estate but it's extremely expensive... Fantastic conditioning and a very good golf course... Better than Loch Lomond and Gleneagles but too expensive... The experience is very average... The round cost a king's ransom but it was worth every cent... One of my favourite days on a golf course ever... Except for the 7th, the course would be totally forgettable in a country of memorable golf courses... Would barely my make Top 15 parkland courses played around the world but good for the British Isles... It's a tough course, you just need to glance back at the championship tees, but playing it off the yellows is a manageable test... You could be on any modern parkland course in the world... I really didn't want the round to end. Oh, to be a millionaire.

Kevin Murray

The K Club, or to give it its full title, the Kildare Country Club, is located in 550 acres of rolling County Kildare countryside. The Palmer course was designed by Arnold Palmer, opening for play in 1991. The River Liffey meanders through the property and becomes hazardous on a number of holes, especially the 8th, where it runs all the way down the left hand side of the fairway.

In October 2006, the K Club played host to the biggest golfing event in Irish history, the 36th Ryder Cup. The Palmer course proved a worthy venue and millions of people witnessed an emotionally charged European Team romp to a record equalling victory – 18½ points to 9½.

You will either love the Palmer course or hate it; you might hate it if you are off your game because it will beat you up viciously, and you'll love it if your game is on song. Either way, no one could dispute that it's a challenging test of golf and it certainly provided plenty of entertainment during the Ryder Cup.

John McHenry – Professional writes:

The K Club Resort boasts two wonderfully compelling Arnold Palmer-designed championship golf courses. The Palmer Course, which hosted the Ryder Cup in 2006, is a rolling parkland layout with the River Liffey as the backdrop. The Palmer has been designed for everyone to enjoy the beautiful landscape that frames the course. Few images are prettier than the walk to the signature 16th island green surrounded by its rich foliage and tranquillity.

The Smurfit Course, host to the Smurfit Kappa European Open, provides the golfer with an altogether different test as this links-styled golf course will demand both accuracy and precision shot making if a good score is to be achieved. Both courses are eco friendly so don't be surprised to have your round disrupted by wandering swans, ducks or pheasants!

Kevin Murray

TRALEE GOLF CLUB
West Barrow, Ardfert, Tralee, Co. Kerry, Ireland
Telephone: +353 (0) 66 713 6379
Website: www.traleegolfclub.com
Architect: Arnold Palmer
Visitors: Open to visitors from May to October

Average Reviewers' Score:

Reviewers' Comments

Wow, what a surprise! Tralee holds your interest all the way round... Underrated... An unforgettable experience... If I were to pick five must-play courses on any visit to Ireland, I would include Tralee... Whole place is beautiful... Two very distinct nines with the first half considerably flatter than the back and this makes the front, dare I say it, easier... The two nines don't fit together very well... Lasting memories are super quick greens... Can't imagine that you will find more spectacular second nine somewhere else... Back nine is simply superb links golf and has become my favourite in all golf, pushing Hillside into second place... Cannot understand the split views on this course but don't let the naysayer discourage you... You'll never forget the second nine holes. Wow, what huge dunes! All par 3s are difficult but great golf-holes... It was in the best shape of any course in the Southwest... Course is tough, but solid golf is rewarded. Add to this the spectacular setting and you have a classic... Overall, a wonderful experience.

Arnold Palmer has designed a course that will stimulate the senses every bit as much as the enchanting and breathtaking scenery. According to folklore, Palmer created the first nine and Mother Nature did the rest. The front nine at Tralee Golf Club plays across fairly level links land, but the majority of the holes hug the coastline and the ground is elevated, affording magnificent views from the cliff top across Tralee Bay to the Atlantic Ocean beyond. The back nine plays through mountainous dunes with fearsome carries across ravines to plateau greens.

The combination and variety of the holes make the entire experience captivating and exciting. There are only a few courses that grab your attention from the first tee shot, keeping hold of it until the very last putt drops. The links at Tralee is one of those few captivating courses.

We always say that the measure of a good golf course is that the holes stay in the memory forever. There are so many memorable holes at Tralee that you might need to throw away some lesser memories to make room for the experience.

David Power – Head Professional writes:

Tralee has received more accolades than a Hollywood blockbuster and the reason is quite simple: the terrain is natural, the ocean views are truly gorgeous – the beach scenes for Ryan's Daughter were filmed to the right of the 2nd hole – there are no gimmicks and the Tralee experience is like no other. Arnold Palmer has created a pure golf course that is playable for the higher handicapper and a stern test for the single digit player.

With holes that sit atop the cliffs and fairways that are routed through and over the gigantic dunes, Tralee is spectacular in every sense. The tower at the back of the 3rd green dates back to the 10th century and the back of the 7th tee overlooks the small harbour that was once a haven for smugglers. The golf course at Tralee may be young but it's already a polished jewel that is set in spectacular scenery steeped in history. Tralee is perhaps the finest test of golf in Ireland.

MOUNT JULIET
Thomastown, County Kilkenny, Ireland
Telephone: +353 (0) 56 777 3064
Website: www.mountjuliet.ie
Architect: Jack Nicklaus
Visitors: Welcome – contact in advance

Average Reviewers' Score:

Reviewers' Comments

What a great parkland course. You have to admire what Nicklaus did at Mount Juliet...
He's created a fun and challenging golf course... We played on a sunny day in April, it was
so much fun although the scores were not too good... Great condition... I thoroughly
enjoyed it and the condition is faultless... No weak holes and many great golf-holes...
Can't fault the greens, they are fabulous and some of the best putting surfaces I've played
on... Greens are enormous and undulating - take plenty of club to avoid coming up
short... Mounds provide good perspective and dimension... A memorable day's golf at an
outstanding resort... Play this course – you won't be disappointed.

The course at Mount Juliet is set in lush, rolling parkland, part of a 1,500 - acre old Irish country estate with an 18th century mansion as the clubhouse. Magnificent mature trees line the fairways. The River Nore cuts through the course and is popular for salmon fishing.

There is a distinctly American feel to this layout, with numerous teeing areas, plenty of bunkers and water hazards. The course can cater for the very best golfers, measuring well over 7,000 yards from the back tees. Three of the world's best have already won the Irish Open here: Faldo (1991), Langer (1992) and Torrance (1993).

Nicklaus has designed a fun golfer's golf course that is eminently playable for the handicap golfer from a choice of forward tees. Water is the main hazard but if you can avoid it, you will have a great time.

Sean Cotter – Head Professional writes:
Mount Juliet is one of the finest parkland courses in Ireland, measuring almost 7,300 yards from the championship tees.

It is a golfer's paradise, which was designed by Jack Nicklaus. It was home to the Carroll's Irish Open in 1993, the Murphy's Irish Open in 1994 and 1995, the Shell Wonderful World of Golf (Tom Watson v Fred Couples) in 1997, Irish Seniors Open in 1999 and the WGC – American Express Championship in 2002 and 2004.

Tiger Woods, who won the 2002 tournament, said: "I think the golf course is absolutely gorgeous, the fairways are perfect, the greens are the best greens we've putted on all year, including the majors – I'm really enjoying being here, it's such a relaxed atmosphere. It is a beautiful place."

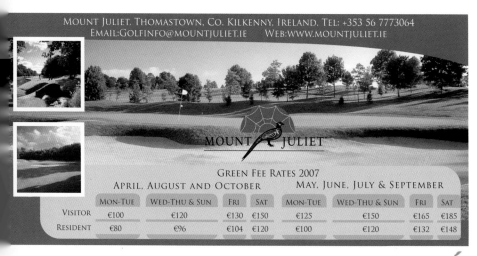

MOUNT JULIET, THOMASTOWN, CO. KILKENNY, IRELAND. TEL: +353 56 7773064
EMAIL:GOLFINFO@MOUNTJULIET.IE   WEB:WWW.MOUNTJULIET.IE

MOUNT JULIET

GREEN FEE RATES 2007

	APRIL, AUGUST AND OCTOBER				MAY, JUNE, JULY & SEPTEMBER			
	MON-TUE	WED-THU & SUN	FRI	SAT	MON-TUE	WED-THU & SUN	FRI	SAT
VISITOR	€100	€120	€130	€150	€125	€150	€165	€185
RESIDENT	€80	€96	€104	€120	€100	€120	€132	€148

GULLANE GOLF CLUB

Gullane, East Lothian, EH31 2BB, Scotland
Telephone: +44 (0) 1620 842255
Website: www.gullanegolfclub.com
Architect: Unknown
Visitors: Book in advance

Average Reviewers' Score:

Reviewers' Comments

Gullane – the best place in Scotland to play golf… No. 1 is a stern and demanding test of golf… Has the most significant elevation changes of any links course in Scotland… Don't bother comparing the three courses just play them all as often as you can! The fun begins at the 2nd which requires a drive uphill to a narrow undulating fairway that is almost impossible to hit directly into the wind… So many great holes: 2nd, 4th, 6th, 7th, and a magnificent sequence round the turn… Just drink in your first view from the top of Gullane Hill… View at the 7th is indescribably stunning, 360 degrees of pure beauty… What a test! You are continually challenged to drive the ball in play to avoid the rough and bunkers which dominate the course… Gullane No.2 is similar, but No.1 is clearly the better course. Both, however, should be on your list of links courses to play… Wonderful golf in the greatest setting.

Steve Burden

Gullane is a small town that lives and breathes golf: there are five superb golf courses in this locality, including the mighty Muirfield. The Gullane No.1 course was laid down in 1884 and is the most senior of a triumvirate of courses at this golf club. Records dating back to 1650 show golf being played over these links, though it is unclear who originally designed the course. Therefore, until we can establish otherwise, we must put it down to Mother Nature.

Gullane is blessed with the most exquisite turf – winter rules are not needed here. If you hit the fairways, a perfect lie awaits, even in the depths of winter. The opening hole, cunningly called "First", is a relatively gentle short par four. The 2nd hole, called "Windygate", begins the march up Gullane Hill. The 3rd hole is called "Racecourse", a short par five which plays along what was once an old 18th century racecourse and it continues to take you onwards and upwards, now at a canter, until you reach the 7th tee and the 200-foot summit of Gullane Hill.

The 360-degree views from the vantage point of the 7th tee are breathtaking. In the foreground, all around are the fluttering flags of Gullane, Muirfield and Luffness New. The Lammermuir Hills lie to the south, while the Firth of Forth wraps up the panorama to the north, west and east. And now, it's time for the 7th and its inviting downhill drive and the scurry home down Gullane Hill.

Alasdair Good – Head PGA Professional writes:
A fair and true test of your links golf skills await here at Gullane. Our fairways are there for all to see but few will successfully manage to navigate the subtle bunkering or penal summer rough that lies in wait.

Rarely will you encounter the variety of shots required to master the changes in elevation and slopes that belie this classic design. When the breeze blows, great imagination rather than strength is called for to record those coveted par figures. Always presented in fine condition with excellent putting surfaces. Take your focus off the course to admire the stunning views at your peril!

COUNTY SLIGO GOLF CLUB

Rosses Point, County Sligo, Ireland
Telephone: +353 (0) 7191 77 134
Website: www.countysligogolfclub.ie   **Architect:** George Combe,
Willie Campbell, Harry Colt and Charles Alison, Martin Hawtree
Visitors: Welcome – contact in advance

Average Reviewers' Score:

Reviewers' Comments

Rosses Point is a classic links course...What a fantastic setting with fantastic views... The scenery is spectacular and if you prefer to play without dunes you'll love this track... The course incorporates some significant elevation changes and beautifully designed holes to produce a fun yet challenging course to play... A quirky opening three holes up and down the hill... After this you turn away from the clubhouse for an adventure into classic linksland and links golf holes... A great elevated driving hole at the 5th, nice loop at the turn between the 9th and 12th then a wonderful series of holes along the coast... I found all the holes interesting, but the 17th may take the cake... Immaculately presented links golf course... Fairways are generously wide and the greens are true and fast... The wind added its expected element of difficulty... Highly recommended... I would visit this course as often as I had the chance... The clubhouse is a very hospitable place to end your round over a jar or two.

Aidan Bradley

County Sligo is an exhilarating west coast links that started out in life as a nine-hole course, designed by George Combe (contriver in 1896 of the world's first handicap system), and opened for play in 1894. At the turn of the 20th century, Willie Campbell extended the course to 18 holes. The famous Colt and Alison partnership remodelled the course in 1927.

There are many spectacular golf courses in Ireland and County Sligo is no exception. The views are simply beautiful and the Ox Mountains – Knockalong the highest peak – add a further dimension to the already stunning vista.

In the same vein as the scenery, County Sligo is a real joy, a strategic links with dramatic undulations, raised plateau greens, run-offs, high ground, low ground, and cliffs, challenging bunkering, burns and dunes. County Sligo has it all, including unusual routing over three distinctly different sections. The back nine, especially the 11th to the 17th, played on the headland, are magnificent. The sheer individuality of holes and the varied terrain makes County Sligo an absolute must-play golf course.

Jim Robinson – Club Professional writes:

County Sligo Golf Club or Rosses Point as its probably better known is a traditional links course with ten holes out to the farthest point from the clubhouse and eight holes back. The golf club was established in 1894 but Harry Colt designed the links we play today in 1927 with a few more improvements over the years by Martin Hawtree whose father worked with Colt, therefore making sure the Colt characteristics are upheld.

Virtually every hole on the course has panoramic views taking in Drumcliff Bay and the beautiful sandy beaches, also Benbulben, Sligo's table top mountain, Lissadell House, former residence of the Countess of Markievicz and Drumcliffe Church where the poet W.B. Yeats is buried. After the golf one should stay locally and sample the excellent pubs and restaurants in the seafaring village of Rosses Point, just to complete the experience.

DRUIDS GLEN GOLF RESORT
Newtownmountkennedy, Co. Wicklow, Ireland
Telephone: +353 (0) 1287 3600
Website: www.druidsglen.ie
Architect: Pat Ruddy and Tom Craddock
Visitors: Book in advance

Average Reviewers' Score:

Reviewers' Comments

Druids Glen is one of my all-time favourite golfing venues and the whole experience is memorable from the moment you arrive until the last pint of Guinness is downed... Whole experience is magnificent and they seemingly have learnt much from the Americans here in terms of service and I mean that positively... Each hole is memorable and the Amen stretch from 12-15 is nothing short of magnificent and the long par 4 13th is my favourite hole in Ireland... 12-14 are really an amen corner and if you can hang it together on these holes then you are doing well... A demanding course, especially from near the back tees but I thoroughly enjoyed myself. My only regret was that I did not have my camera to hand... Feels as though you are taking a walk in someone's private manicured garden which is packed full of specimen trees (8th and 12th are perfect examples of this)... A first class course and a wonderful resort... A world-class course without a shadow of doubt and I can't wait to return... Druids Glen should not be missed.

Druids Glen

Druids Glen is a unique golfing experience, derived from Ruddy and Craddock's inspired design. The ambience is distinguished and distinctly Irish, including an ancient druids' altar located behind the 12th green. The views are pretty pleasing too and the challenge is not insignificant, but if you can keep on the immaculate and generous fairways, scoring well will become a real possibility. This is target golf country, from the perfect fairway lie to a huge soft green where putting on the immaculate surface is an absolute joy. But don't be fooled by this, there are many varied challenges at Druids Glen, not least the threatening water, which seems to be everywhere. If you're not on top of your game, it can be a brutal course.

After a strong start and a tough Amen Corner after the turn, Druids Glen closes in a blaze of glory. The 17th will put fear into all but the most confident golfer. It's a 203-yard par three to an island green – let's hope it's not too windy. The closing hole measures 450 yards and there's water all around the approach to the green. There is no doubt that Druids Glen will remain etched in the memory for a long time. Make sure that you take enough golf balls with you.

George Henry – Golf Professional writes:
Druids Glen, a highly acclaimed parkland masterpiece set in the heart of famous County Wicklow, is styled as "The Augusta of Europe".

This world-class course has gained huge international recognition having hosted the prestigious Irish Open four times during the 1990s and The Seve Trophy in 2002.

Druids Glen, co-designed in the mid-1990s by Pat Ruddy and former Walker Cup player Tom Craddock, is a fascinating challenge which takes golfers on a magical journey through one of Ireland's great estates with the Wicklow countryside and Irish Sea serving as a spectacular backdrop.

It is a championship course presented in tournament condition which evokes happy memories for several top players including Colin Montgomerie, Sergio Garcia and Seve Ballesteros, who showered praise on the course in their victory speeches.

Druids Glen

GLENEAGLES HOTEL
Auchterarder, Perthshire, PH3 1NF, Scotland
Telephone: +44 (0) 1764 662231
Website: www.gleneagles.com
Architect: James Braid
Visitors: Book at least 8 weeks in advance

Average Reviewers' Score:

Reviewers' Comments

The Queen's may be the most beautiful place to play golf in the world... If this course was a baby you would pinch its cheek and say, "Oh you lovely, cute, sweet, little baby" and possibly blow on its tummy at this stage! Course is first class and I remain unsure as to whether I enjoyed it more than the King's – that's how good it is... Sun glistens through the trees, deer appear on the fairway, birds swoop and soar and the views of the surrounding hills are simply lovely... I love this course and I rate it second to only the Ailsa at Turnberry, and that said, the two are far from comparable... The Queen's is a perfect club golfer's track, short enough to allow you to score, and pristine enough to let you know you are playing at a world-class venue... Biggest differential between the halves of any course I know. Back 9 is about six shots easier but both are crammed with interesting and challenging holes, notably the par threes... Experience is a golfing treat as well as an aesthetic one... Enjoy all the qualities of Gleneagles on this beautiful course.

Anthony Munter

The Queen's course is the pretty little sister at Gleneagles. The holes are set within an altogether softer landscape than the King's and PGA Centenary courses. She's only a short course and not the most challenging, but she is exquisitely delicate and stunningly beautiful.

Designed by James Braid, the Queen's course opened for play in 1917. From the medal tees, the course measures less than 6,000 yards, but with a lowly par of 68, it represents an immensely enjoyable challenge. This is one of the finest parcels of golfing land in the British Isles. The holes weave their way across undulating moorland, through charming woodland, to greens set in pretty glades. The ball sits proudly on the springy fairways, inviting the most solid strike. The greens are true and ideal for bold putting and this really is an enchanting and exhilarating place to play golf.

Gleneagles is unusual in that it has three different golf courses and it's also unique because it's the only place in Scotland to have three inland courses and they have all appeared in recent ranking lists. But above all, this is a place to enjoy the entertainment and have some fun.

Russell Smith – Head Professional writes:
The natural beauty of the Queen's Course inspires the world's most experienced players. In its long history, the Queen's has played host to some of the world's golfing greats.

Threading through high ridges on the north and west sides of the estate, the Queen's offers lovely woodland settings, lochans and ditches as water hazards, as well as many moorland characteristics. At 3,192 yards long, the challenge of the first nine can be deceptive, with even some of the best players finding it a test to make par into a fresh southwesterly breeze.

The key challenge on the Queen's is accuracy. In particular, the par threes on the back nine require precision shot-making to find the greens with your tee shot.

Anthony Munter

THE ISLAND GOLF CLUB
Corballis, Donabate, Co. Dublin, Ireland
Telephone: +353 (0) 1843 6205
Website: www.theislandgolfclub.com
Architect: Fred Hawtree & Eddie Hackett, Jeff Howes
Visitors: Contact in advance

Average Reviewers' Score:

Reviewers' Comments

One of the best links courses around... The Island was more fun than any course we've played in Ireland or Scotland... It's an amazing old-fashioned links course that is basically surrounded by water... Huge dunes, rolling fairways, deep bunkers and tricky greens... As great as the course is, the real winners are the vistas and the terrain... A real cracker of an opening hole and, to be honest, the 15th would get on many 'best links hole' surveys... On the front nine you play through a series of canyons through the sand hills. The back nine is more open. It makes you feel like you're the only ones on the course and the views out to sea are just awesome... Some holes like the 3rd & the monster 18th require very accurate long approaches... A few holes have some giant dunes as a background and, for me, the front nine is the best, especially closing in around the turn... Accurate driving is a must and holes you think you should score well on don't always work out that way... Every shot definitely requires you to think... This course has it all.

The Island in Ireland was once on an island. It's now attached to the mainland but it's still an isolated peninsula-like spur of links land, sandwiched between the Irish Sea, the beach of Donabate and the Broadmeadow estuary.

Few people know about The Island Golf Club, despite the fact that the course is over one hundred years old and has featured in numerous ranking tables over the years.

Bernard Darwin was certainly aware at the turn of the 20th century because in his book, The Golf Courses of the British Isles, he wrote extensively about Royal Dublin and Portmarnock and said: "It would be unfair to omit some mention of Malahide – 'the Island' – where there is golf to be had, which may legitimately be called sporting in the best sense of the word."

This is a no-frills golf course. There is nothing manicured and it's all very harmonious and in tune with its surroundings. Some of the most shaggy, rugged and looming sand dunes imaginable provide natural and distinct amphitheatres for many of the holes. In the summer, if you are unfortunate and wayward enough to find the dunes, be careful to avoid trampling on the wild dune flowers. The club is quite rightly proud of its flora. Expect to hear the hypnotic song of the lark – there are plenty to be heard and the skylark is the Island's club emblem.

James W. Finegan writes:
The Island is a great course, compelling our respect for the testing quality of its holes, winning our admiration for its naturalness, endowing us from start to finish with unique joy of seaside golf at its best. The world should be beating a path to its door.

Royal St David's

ROYAL ST DAVID'S GOLF CLUB
Harlech, Gwynedd, LL46 2UB, Wales
Telephone: +44 (0) 1766 780361
Website: www.royalstdavids.co.uk
Architect: Harold Finch-Hatton, William Henry More
Visitors: Current handicap required – book in advance

Average Reviewers' Score:

Reviewers' Comments

Harlech is a daunting proposition from the moment you turn up... Superb championship links course, a real test of golf... Without doubt a long tough test of golf and a must-do golfing experience... Quality and condition of the greens is always first rate... The fairway bunkering is spot on and to make a good score, avoid these off the tee... Plays as two very different nines... Front nine has a number of holes that are rather forgetful... Score well on the front, as the back plays into the breeze and a lot of the par 4s are unreachable in two shots... Best hole is without doubt the 15th – a great par 4! Back nine bobs and weaves its way through sand dunes... Dunes come into play on the 14th, 15th and 16th... One of the finest back nines in all golf... Really difficult par 69 layout... The clubhouse is fine and the Secretary was very welcoming.

Royal St David's Golf Club

The glorious setting for the Royal St David's links at Harlech is nothing short of beautiful and romantic. The forbidding medieval Harlech castle and towering sand dunes guard the course. Behind the dunes, to the northwest, is the sweeping bay of Tremedog and to the north are views across to Snowdon and the lesser peaks of Snowdonia.

Locals regard Royal St David's as the world's toughest par 69. Who would argue with them? The course measures 6,500 yards from the back tees. It's not your usual out-and-back links – the holes zigzag in all directions, subjecting each shot to the vagaries of the prevailing westerly wind.

The opening dozen holes are fully exposed to the elements. They play back and forth across fairly flat and at times, open ground. When the 13th hole is reached, the landscape changes dramatically and at last we enter rippling undulating dune land. Unusually, Royal St David's closes out with a tough 200-yard par three with the green directly in front of the clubhouse.

John Barnett – Professional writes:
"A past Club President once described Royal St David's as a 'magical place' and, having been the Professional here for over 30 years, I can only agree.

It is set out below Harlech castle on natural reclaimed links land. It has only two par fives playing in opposite directions, five par threes of varying length and difficulty and eleven par fours going in all directions, of which seven are well over 400 yards. It is a typical links, flat and deceptive in length, with fast large greens, which are in wonderful condition all year round.

After playing a testing front nine going in all directions, you then turn into the prevailing wind with a tough 10th hole measuring over 450 yards and a back nine with a lowly par of 33. It is probably the toughest par 69 you will ever play."

Royal St David's Golf Club

WENTWORTH CLUB

Virginia Water, Surrey, GU25 4LS, England
Telephone: +44 (0) 1344 842201
Website: www.wentworthclub.com
Architect: Harry Colt
Visitors: Handicap certificate required – contact in advance

Average Reviewers' Score:

Reviewers' Comments

The beauty of the East course is that it gives you all the style and quality of the West but you have a fairer chance of playing to your handicap… It seems more natural and definitely prettier than the West… What a treat it was – like most things at Wentworth, it has got style and class… For winter golf it takes a lot of beating… Shorter than its illustrious counterpart but still as tight, just as pretty and a lot less busy… Fairly short in places… Par 3s are all varied and testing… The 11th is one of the great par 4s, left to right off the tee, across classic Colt bunkers followed by a right to left draw into a tiered green… It's hard to believe when you play it that there are two other courses so close by… Add the East to your list of courses to play… Don't rush to Wentworth and make straight for the West, this course is equally worth the money… If you get an invitation grab it, and it's a darn sight cheaper in the winter.

Kevin Murray

The West is the course that everybody rushes to play, but the East is more sandy, intimate and charming.

In terms of length, it's relatively short, measuring 6,200 yards from the back tees, but it's an exceedingly pleasant walk on the springy turf and the lowly par of 68 will make playing to handicap a serious challenge. There's only one par five, but there are five par fours measuring in excess of 400 yards. It's the East's collection of five short holes that stand out: they are simply outstanding par threes.

The East course occupies the central area of the Wentworth estate with the newer Edinburgh course now sitting on the eastern side. It is a very special and intimate experience, as many people will already know. The enclosed woodland setting confuses your sense of direction – where only one hole is generally in view and they seem to zigzag all over the place. It always comes as a pleasant surprise when we reach the halfway house where we can have a drink and draw a deep breath before we take on the 7th, an appealing, but challenging, long par three.

The late Michael Williams former Telegraph Golf Correspondent:
Though perhaps overshadowed by the major events that are held on the West, Wentworth's East course is, in fact, the senior of the two.

The existing first hole on the West, which is sometimes referred to as the Burma Road, was the original opening hole on the East, the second then being played to the East's present first green. Otherwise the two courses have always gone their separate ways. While Wentworth's East is much shorter with a standard scratch score of 70 as opposed the West's 74, it is a first class course in its own right and, to perhaps the less able golfers, probably more enjoyable.

NOTTS GOLF CLUB

Hollinwell, Kirby-in-Ashfield, Nottinghamshire, NG17 7QR, England
Telephone: +44 (0) 1623 753225
Website: www.nottsgolfclub.co.uk
Architect: Willie Park Jnr, John H. Taylor
Visitors: Contact in advance – weekdays only – handicap cert required

Average Reviewers' Score:

Reviewers' Comments

One of the unsung gems of inland golf... Fantastic variation with holes cut through valleys and elevated tee shots galore... It now measures a whopping 7,213 yards from the blue tees... This course is unbelievably difficult... 2nd and 3rd holes are the pick of the front nine with the 3rd green by the clubhouse... Smooth fast and true greens, narrow fairways and wicked wispy rough make Notts a course suited to the low handicapper... Each hole has its own features and charms, and as you walk round the golf course, you never want the round to end... Do take a look at the wonderful par 13th from that top back tee... Greens were as good as any I have played but beware of the speed and undulations... A dream for very good putters... Very fair test of golf... Clubhouse is one of the best I've been in, very old and spacious with plenty of interesting photos and trophies... Highly recommended and reasonably priced.

Notts Golf Club is also known as Hollinwell because there is a holy well located amongst the trees close to the 8th fairway. Water from the well is said to lend much needed strength to the golfer, especially during the heat of summer. One of the British Isles' finest inland golf courses, Notts opened for play in 1887, originally designed by Willie Park Jnr. Modifications (primarily to bunkering) were later made by John H Taylor, to whom the club paid the princely sum of five guineas for his services!

The course plays across wonderfully undulating ground where some of the fairways sweep through wooded hillsides and where others run through heather, fern and gorse clad valleys. Unusually, there are a number of varieties of gorse at Notts, and even in the depths of winter, you will find some in flower.

Notts feels very much like heathland (the soil is sandy and the turf is spongy), but it also has a moorland flavour and a touch of woodland. Despite the varied landscape, this attractive course comes together really well and actually gets better and better as you progress from hole to hole. It is also worth mentioning that a great deal of effort is being put in to encourage the heather to return to its former glory.

The following passage was published in Henry Cotton's Guide to Golf In The British Isles and was written by David Talbot, who was then the club professional: "I would describe Holinwell – which is the popular name for the club – as a severe heathland type course: Played from the Championship tees it presents a formidable test for professionals and the top amateurs; the medal tees give a very interesting but slightly shorter course for the club competitions.

The best hole on the course is the 227-yard 14th, played from a high tee down a valley, at the foot of which is the green. The chief danger here is to underestimate the distance and be short."

BALLYLIFFIN GOLF CLUB

Ballyliffin, Inishowen, Co. Donegal, Ireland
Telephone: +353 (0) 7493 76119
Website: www.ballyliffingolfclub.com
Architect: Pat Ruddy, Tom Craddock
Visitors: Welcome – contact in advance

Average Reviewers' Score:

Reviewers' Comments

One of the most enjoyable courses I have played... my favourite in the area... everything you would want from a modern golf links... Glashedy is a great test... bunkers seem to gather nearly good shots and punish you heavily... towering dunes lining the holes... when the wind blows, playing to your handicap is a mean achievement... you have to think your way round... layout is great with lots of elevation... certainly sharpens your short game... the location is fantastic... is a delight both visually and in golfing terms... only weak hole was No.7... cannot speak highly enough about the warmth of the welcome and enjoyment of both courses... the clubhouse was the best I visited of all the West Ireland courses... excellent value for money... I will definitely be back... a must-play if you're in the North... it's a hike to get here because of its remoteness but for pure golf fans like me who travel far and wide to play the best courses, it's worth it.

Ballyliffin Golf Club

Ballyliffin is Ireland's most northerly golf club, located off Tullagh Point on the Atlantic edge of the Inishowen Peninsula. It's difficult to pin a date on the earliest origins of the game of golf at Ballyliffin, but the Ballyliffin Golf Club was founded in 1947. The Glashedy links is, however, much, much younger.

Pat Ruddy and Tom Craddock were commissioned to design a new course on the finest links land they had ever seen. Work started in spring 1993, and after significant earth-moving, the Glashedy links (pronounced Glasheedy) – named after the Glashedy Rock, Ballyliffin's equivalent of Turnberry's Ailsa Craig – opened for play in the summer of 1995, to much acclaim.

The Glashedy layout is intertwined with the Old course, the holes weaving their way through the wild dunes. It's a supremely challenging golf course which stretches out more than 7,200 yards, with nine brutal par fours in excess of 400 yards. You really do need to be on top of your game to play to handicap. The huge greens, with some frightening undulations, are well protected by bunkers; three putting can be alarmingly frequent.

John P Dolan – PGA Head Professional writes:

The Glashedy Links at Ballyliffin Golf Club is renowned as one of the finest pure links tests of golf. Set on the outer boundaries of its sister course – The Old Links – on the north coast of Ireland, Glashedy has panoramic views of the Atlantic Ocean and the rolling hills of Donegal. Standing on the first tee you know that they you are in for a memorable day's golf.

Some of the key holes on the course are the 5th, a 173-yard par three guarded by four pot bunkers, the par three, 7th with its view from the tee box for miles around, the par five 13th, 564 yards up through the dunes to an elevated green and the index 1, 15th with its three pot bunkers guarding the entrance to the green.

The Glashedy Links is without a weak hole and this is what makes it a must-visit for golfers from all corners of the world.

Ballyliffin Golf Club

THE BERKSHIRE GOLF CLUB
Swinley Road, Ascot, Berkshire, SL5 8AY, England
Telephone: +44 (0) 1344 621495
Website: None
Architect: Herbert Fowler
Visitors: By prior arrangement

Average Reviewers' Score:

Reviewers' Comments
Great club, much friendlier than 'stuffy' Sunningdale… Wonderful course but it needs to be played more than once… The Red is definitely the better of the two courses, which are tough to spilt after the first visit… Both courses are great value and nobody I know who has played here has been disappointed… The Red is tighter and more intimate… Each hole is separated from the rest by the forest and each and every one of them is stunning… Many people claim that the Red and the Blue make up the finest 36-hole heathland combination in the world… The combination of six par threes, fours and fives is entertainment but it's the outstanding par threes which will stick in the mind… The par 3s are phenomenal… If you only have time for one round, make sure you play the Red rather than the Blue. The Red is a classic.

Andy Taylor

Many people say that there is nothing better than a day's golf amongst the forest, heather and springy turf of the Berkshire Golf Club. Both the Red and the Blue courses are charming. The Red course is considered to be the more senior of the two, but frankly there is little to choose between them.

Herbert Fowler, who had a gift for blending golf courses into their natural surroundings, laid out both courses in 1928. Fowler clearly did a great job because only minor changes have since been made to his original design. The land was once the hunting forest of the royals and dates back to the reign of Queen Anne. Each hole is played in seclusion, the mature sycamore, birch, chestnut and pine trees providing majestic tunnels for the rippled fairways.

The Red acquired its name from a military analogy with the Blue taking the opposite side. The Red course is highly unusual in design. The configuration of six par threes, six par fives and six par fours provide for much interest, variety and entertainment.

The Red's hallmark is most definitely the six par threes – they are all superb in their own right. Actually, we think that this a fantastic golf course and will provide a memorable day out for any serious golfer.

Paul Anderson – Head Professional writes:
I can't think of a better day's golfing than to play the Red and Blue courses at The Berkshire Golf Club. Just be careful not to eat too much lunch, otherwise you might not be able to appreciate the course in the afternoon!

Both courses are as wonderful as each other, with mature pine trees, heather and excellent greens combining to provide a picturesque yet testing day's golf.

Andy Taylor

NEFYN & DISTRICT GOLF CLUB
Morfa Nefyn, Pwllheli, Gwynedd, LL53 6DA, Wales
Telephone: +44 (0) 1758 720966
Website: www.nefyn-golf-club.com
Architect: J.H. Taylor and James Braid
Visitors: Contact in advance

Average Reviewers' Score:

Reviewers' Comments

It is impossible for spirits to be dampened on a layout like this... You have to pinch yourself to believe it's really true... Really good, a great day had by all – the views are magic and each hole is very different... Fantastic cliff top course... Final 8 holes on the Old course cannot be bettered... Scenery is something out of a film set, looking out over the bay to massive volcano-like mountains climbing out of the sea... 2nd hole gives a true taste of what's to come - a drive out over the rocks and the sea to a fairway that snakes along the cliff edge. This is one of, if not *the* most spectacular tee shot in Wales... Sequence of holes from 14 to 17 is breathtaking and offers a unique experience... It's just so different... When you've finished the golf, the hospitality is second to none... Truly awesome, unique, spectacular and the most memorable course I've ever played... Will certainly be returning in the near future... A MUST for everyone.

Nefyn is dramatically located on the cliff tops at the foot of the Porthdinllaen headland, a tiny promontory that juts out from the Lleyn Peninsula into the Irish Sea. In terms of sheer exhilaration, Nefyn is Wales' equivalent of Ireland's Old Head of Kinsale. This is literally golf on the edge of the world and it makes the adrenaline pump.

Nefyn and District Golf Club was founded in 1907, originally as a nine-hole course and in 1912, it was extended to 18 holes. Two of the great triumvirate, J.H. Taylor and James Braid were commissioned in 1933 to add a further nine and to revise the existing course.

Today's layout is extremely unusual because only 26 holes are now in play. We have a feeling that one of the holes fell into the sea. The course now comprises 10 outward holes and two separate inward 8 holes. They call the two courses the Old and the New.

There are only a few seaside courses where you can see the sea from every hole, but you sure can at Nefyn. Not only is the sea in view, but also on a clear day, you can spot peaks of the Wicklow Mountains across the Irish Sea.

John Froom – Professional writes:
Nefyn & District Golf Club will appeal to all golfers who enjoy a challenging course. It offers a tantalising mixture of exciting holes requiring a variety of shot-making skills and a very steady nerve to score well. The course is set against the scenic backdrop of spectacular mountains and breathtaking coastline.

With a unique 26-hole layout this includes perhaps the most frequently photographed eight holes in UK golf – the world famous 'Point' – routed along a pencil-thin promontory jutting into the sea. Take on the early challenge of driving across the coves and inlets of the coastline before turning inland to tackle some demanding par fours and fives. Then set off along the stretch known as Wales's own 'Pebble Beach'. Nefyn has something to offer and reward every standard of golfer. It's a never-to-be forgotten experience.

ROSAPENNA GOLF RESORT
Downings, Letterkenny, Co. Donegal, Ireland
Telephone: +353 (0) 74 915 5301
Website: www.rosapennagolflinks.ie
Architect: Pat Ruddy
Visitors: Welcome – contact in advance

Average Reviewers' Score:

Reviewers' Comments

Sandy Hills is an outstanding, and most importantly, complete golf course... Dune structure of this virgin property is the best in Ireland and the architect Pat Ruddy has used it to perfection... One of the most exacting tests of golf I have ever played, but in such stunningly beautiful surroundings it is a joyful struggle... A fun course for the golf addict and the dune junky... From 1 to hole 18, there is not a weak hole... Ruddy is the Irish golfing magician with the ability to create big dipper, thrill-a-minute, links golf in and amongst the most inhospitable of terrain... Bunkers are sometimes hidden from view... Most holes enjoy the isolation of their own little valley through the dunes... My only criticism is the rock hard greens... A truly mammoth challenge even in calm conditions... The most dramatic and well routed new course in Ireland in the past decade... Of all the courses I played in West Ireland, it is this course that would draw me back again...True heavenly links.

Rosapenna Golf Resort

The pretty fishing village of Downings lies on the edge of Sheep Haven Bay in the north of Donegal, a county that is rapidly becoming one of Ireland's best golfing destinations.

Golf at Rosapenna dates back to 1891. But it was Pat Ruddy, the man behind the European Club, who put Rosapenna firmly on the map. His new course, Sandy Hills, will surely end up on every serious golfer's must-play list.

Sandy Hills quietly opened for play in June 2003 and slowly, but surely, the golfing world is beginning to recognise that this course is special. Old Tom chose to route the Old course alongside the dunes, but Pat Ruddy had different ideas – he decided to carve straight through them and this is presumably how the name Sandy Hills came into being. Right from the off, you are in a lunar landscape, amongst the gigantic dunes. Going over and through the dunes provides a platform to drink in the stunning views across the Old course to Sheep Haven Bay beyond. It's spectacular.

Bryan Patterson – Head Professional writes:
Had Robert Louis Stevenson visited North West Donegal before he discovered the Monterey Peninsula, Sandy Hills and not Pebble Beach would be basking in his immortal words "the greatest meeting place of land and sea".

For golfers who enjoy playing their golf by the sea, Sandy Hills is absolute heaven. So much so that I am sure the good Lord knew something about links golf.

I hesitate to highlight particular holes as this may suggest the remainder are less equal – but not so here. Variety is the thing which stretches the visitor. The opening holes play along the beautiful Tramore Beach (Stevenson would have loved them) and you then turn for home through the majestic Rosapenna Dunes. The spectacular views of Mulroy Bay make the Sandy Hills Links a contender for the top of any serious golfers itinerary.

Rosapenna Hotel & Golf Links
Where the waters meet the wild and 4 star luxury nestles amidst the rolling Donegal landscape.

Tranquil lounges and elegant dining areas create a congenial atmosphere and a perfect place for visitors to relax and enjoy themselves. Guests unwind in the hotel's swimming pool, whirlpool and steam room.

ROYAL CINQUE PORTS GOLF CLUB
Golf Road, Deal, Kent, CT14 6RF, England
Telephone: +44 (0) 1304 374007
Website: www.royalcinqueports.com
Architect: Henry Hunter, James Braid, Sir Guy Campbell
Visitors: Contact in advance – Not Wed am or at weekend

Average Reviewers' Score:

Reviewers' Comments

A truly first class links... Tremendous history of Open Championships and Amateur Championships and its fearsome reputation is well deserved... New tees and bunker refurbishment have really improved this great course... If you want towering dunes and scenic beauty, forget Deal. However, those students of links golf who thrive on tight lies, rolling fairways, deep riveted bunkers and quick true greens will have a day to remember... Course is an hourglass in shape and the bit in the middle is quite dramatic with fairways and greens draped over the dunes... Front 9 isn't excessively long and it is here that you must try and make your score... From the 12th the stakes are raised and the homeward stretch is absolutely brutal... Links golf of the highest calibre and the 15th, 16th and 17th wouldn't look out of place on any of the courses of the current Open Championship rota... Top class championship links golf at a reasonable price... Wow – links golf as it should be played... Would not hesitate to play it again... Wonderful!

Kevin Murray

Royal Cinque Ports, or Deal as it is more commonly known, is a brutal links course. Its back nine, or rather the last seven holes, are relentless, invariably playing directly into the teeth of the prevailing south westerly wind. The layout is stark and cheerless – only the sandhills and wild dune grasses provide this narrow out-and-back layout with any real definition. You can expect tight and hanging lies from the fairways, making stances awkward. Let's make no bones about it – this is a tough course. Make your score on the front nine, otherwise Deal can make even the very best golfers look like weekend duffers.

In 1909, J. H. Taylor – one of the Great Triumvirate – proudly won the first Open ever played at Royal Cinque Ports. The Open returned to Deal in 1920 and made Walter Hagen look decidedly useless. In the lead-up to the Open, Hagen had boasted that he was unbeatable. He eventually ended up in 55th place!

1920 was to be the last Open held at Deal, despite the fact that it was planned to return in 1949, but sadly the sea breached its defences and flooded the course.

Andrew Reynolds – Head Professional writes:
Deal is one of nature's masterpieces, as natural a course as you can find. Situated on an undulating stretch of sandhills, it follows the sea on its outward nine and when the holes reach our 'bottom end', you play straight back to the clubhouse.

This true links course is a severe battle – a shorter front nine with the testing back nine played into the prevailing wind. The giant slick greens will test the best and you will leave your day with an eager desire to return. Your memories will be of a course surrounded by the biggest sky and an even bigger test of your golf.

THE BLAIRGOWRIE GOLF CLUB
Golf Course Road, Rosemount, Blairgowrie, Perthshire, PH10 6LG, Scotland
Telephone: +44 (0) 1250 872622
Website: www.theblairgowriegolfclub.co.uk
Architect: Dr Alister MacKenzie, James Braid
Visitors: Welcome – contact in advance

Average Reviewers' Score:

Reviewers' Comments

Blairgowrie is a delightful place to spend some time... A tree-lined course with superb greens which is always in excellent condition... Course was in great shape for the time of year... Easy to walk... The Rosemount has wider fairways than the neighbouring Lansdowne course but both are similar with a mix of tricky par 3s, birdieable par 5s and difficult par 4s... I didn't remove the driver from my golf bag once all day as it is so important – with trees lining most holes – to keep the ball in play... Every tee offers a similar challenge (thread drive between tall trees) and the flatness of it all gives sameness to the experience... The beauty of Rosemount is that while each hole may be hard to recall, the overall experience is fantastic and the new club house has brought top level facilities to the after-golf experience as well... Decent golf course and well manicured... The best holes are 1, 16 and 17... Very good course(s) that you should play and a welcome change from the links!

Blairgowrie Golf Club

Blairgowrie Golf Club is charmingly situated at the feet of the Grampian Mountains amongst glorious pine, birch and heather. The club was founded in 1889 when a nine-hole course was laid out close to the Black Loch on land owned by the Marchioness of Lansdowne.

Dr Alister MacKenzie was commissioned to extend the course to 18 holes in 1914, but the Great War delayed the opening until 1927. Then, in the 1930s, James Braid was called in to add a further nine holes and create a new 18-hole layout. Today's Rosemount is therefore a James Braid design with a sprinkling of Alister MacKenzie. The original nine-hole course remains and it's a charming 2,327-yard heathland track called the Wee.

The Rosemount is definitely a very pretty and classy inland course, the crisp turf has a moorland feel to it with the fairways pitching and rolling through avenues of trees. Each hole is carved through the trees, which provide a natural amphitheatre for a calm and tranquil round of golf.

From start to finish the holes are good and varied, but the best holes are left until last. The 17th is especially noteworthy, a lovely par three called "Plateau" with a two-tiered green. The pro's tip is to take plenty of club, to get on the right level and avoid three putts.

Charles Dernie – Head Professional writes:
Rosemount is unique in Scottish golf, being a genuine heathland course. The generous and beautifully maintained fairways wend their way through lovely Scots pine and heather – but keep on the short grass or your score may rocket!

Deer, red squirrels and pheasants abound and you would be hard pressed to find a better finish. Blairgowrie is a delight to play.

CARTON HOUSE
Maynooth, Co. Kildare, Ireland
Telephone: +353 (0) 1 505 2000
Website: www.carton.ie
Architect: Colin Montgomerie and Stan Eby
Visitors: Welcome – contact in advance

Average Reviewers' Score:

Reviewers' Comments

As an inland links, it has no equal in Ireland... If you like the going tough, then the Monty course is for you... If you like brilliantly conditioned courses, fast greens, great service and a seriously difficult test of golf then this course will tick all those boxes... Played last week off the white pegs in a slight wind, easily the hardest golf course I have ever played... This course should be in the Top 100 on pure merit... Greens are excellent with lovely rolling fairways... There are 145 bunkers – some 10-feet deep – you have to stay out of them... A wonderful course, with a good second course in the O'Meara... Superb condition, no weak holes and a great clubhouse... Another must play course from my week in Ireland.

Carton House

Located a mere 15 miles to the west of Dublin city centre, Carton House is set to become a popular golfing destination. The 1,100-acre walled Carton Estate dates back to Norman times and a new luxury four-star hotel is currently being built in sympathy with Carton House, the existing ancient mansion. Carton House is not only located in a beautiful setting, but it's easily accessible.

There are two courses, the more senior O'Meara, which opened for play in 2002 and the Montgomerie, which opened the following year. Both are contrasting in style: the O'Meara is park-like and the Montgomerie links-like. This is the second course to be designed by "Monty" and he was helped and guided by Stan Eby of European Golf Design. It's an interesting sculptured layout which stretches out to a massive 7,300 yards from the championship tees.

Without huge defining sand dunes, links- type courses can be flat and featureless. The Montgomerie course gets its definition from manufactured undulations; swaying fescue grass, clear definition between the cuts of grass and the many deep pot bunkers. It clearly has a modern look and feel but it's an honest an unpretentious driver's course which hangs together rather well. There is no signature hole to speak of, just one good hole after another, and the par threes are especially noteworthy.

Francis Howley – Golf Professional
The Montgomerie Course at Carton House is home to the 2004 AIB Irish Amateur Open Championship and the 2005 & 2006 Nissan Irish Open. Designed by its namesake, Colin Montgomerie, it presents the golfer with a very different challenge of head high pot bunkers, fast running greens and narrow fairways weaving through fields of fescue grasses.

Though an inland layout, the Montgomerie plays very much like a links course in that the fairways are rolling, the rough is incredibly tough and there are virtually no trees. Add to the mixture well over 100 exceptionally well-positioned and often cavernous bunkers and you will only begin to appreciate the quality of this course.

COUNTY LOUTH GOLF CLUB
Baltray, Drogheda, County Louth, Ireland
Telephone: +353 (0) 41 988 1530
Website: www.countylouthgolfclub.com
Architect: Tom Simpson
Visitors: Contact in advance – not Tuesdays

Average Reviewers' Score:

Reviewers' Comments
One of the true hidden gems in golf… Remote location only adds to the charm… There's a reason for Baltray to be "Ireland's most overlooked links", it's shockingly overpriced… An understated classic links, which will test the best golfers… There are no tricks and few really memorable holes but there is not one single weak hole… Good, not great, holes, with penal rough and a similarity of design throughout… Very welcoming course which is 100% links in nature but with only 3-4 really great holes to get the heartbeat elevated… A number of elevated tee shots and greens that are tucked away here and there… Front nine isn't too difficult and is pretty flat… Back moves closer to the water and into some bigger dunes and that is where the better holes are located… It's reputed to have the best greens in Ireland and I've played here three times and I can't disagree… Make sure you book in advance… Baltray is a course to savour and enjoy.

Aidan Bradley

There is generally a certain level of anticipation when one plays a course for the first time. The approach road to the links of County Louth, or Baltray as it is better known, named after the local fishing village, is especially uplifting. This is a course that has remained relatively anonymous, except to those in the know. It is one of Ireland's secrets.

County Louth Golf Club was established in 1892 but Tom Simpson designed the present course in 1938. In 2003, Tom MacKenzie made some minor changes to the layout, most notably the addition of new tees, which has stretched the yardage beyond 7,000 yards.

Darren Clarke won the East of Ireland Championship in 1989, an amateur stroke play event held at County Louth since 1941, although it is unlikely that anybody will beat Joe Carr's record. Joe Carr was the "East" champion 12 times between 1941 and 1969. Amazingly, Joe's son Roddy won the 1970 "East" championship.

Baltray has no weak holes. The course is laid out in two loops, and most holes run in different directions. However, the greens are County Louth's hallmark – they are among the very best in the whole of Ireland. If you can avoid three putting for 18 holes, then you have the right to claim you're a great putter.

Although County Louth is a championship links golf course, golfers of all levels can enjoy it. The back nine is especially entertaining with a number of holes running close to the shore with distant views towards the Mountains of Mourne. County Louth hosted the Nissan Irish Open in July 2004.

James W. Finegan – extract from Emerald Fairways and Foam-Flecked Seas:
Let it be said at once: Baltray is a great and glorious course, a classic sandhill layout with consistently high shot values, admiral variety, moments of tension and of beauty. What's more, its greens are among the very best – and most creatively contoured – in Ireland.

County Louth Golf Club

PENNARD GOLF CLUB
2 Southgate Road, Southgate, Swansea, SA3 2BT, Wales
Telephone: +44 (0) 1792 233131
Website: www.pennardgolfclub.com
Architect: James Braid, Ken Cotton
Visitors: Welcome – contact in advance

Average Reviewers' Score:

Reviewers' Comments

Pennard was the highlight of our trip… Challenging, rugged, natural and the Real McCoy! Without doubt the gem in the crown of Welsh golf courses… Very quirky design will split opinion… It provided our group with a very stern challenge… Plenty of elevated greens where you need to take at least one more club and if you miss in the wrong place a tricky up and down will follow… Views from nearly every point on this course are superb, in particular the 7th green and the 16th tee… 7th, with the ruins of an old church and castle will remain etched in my mind for a very long time indeed – what a classic… At times you just don't know where you are going but who cares when the views are just magic – sea, beach, cliffs and a castle… People were friendly, the food and beer was great… All in all a superb day out and a fabulous place to test your game and in particular your nerves… One thing's for sure, you'll never forget Pennard.

Pennard is set on the rugged Gower Peninsula, amongst one of the most dramatic landscapes in Britain. Its cliff-top site provides an ideal vantage point – from the heights, the views across to the beautiful sandy beaches of Three Cliff and Oxwich Bays are simply arresting.

Pennard is one of the oldest golf courses in Wales. Reputedly, golf has been played here since 1896, although the Pennard Golf Club was not founded until 1908. It's often called "the links in the sky", because the holes play across links-like ground, full of dunes, humps and hollows but the land is 200 feet above sea level.

When the strong winds funnel up the Bristol Channel, it will pose a stern challenge to the very best golfers. Don't let your concentration be affected by the wild ponies and cattle, which graze on the links. Additionally, expect a few blind shots and don't expect too many flat lies – Pennard is seriously hilly, with more ups and downs than most links courses, but we think it's a delightful old-fashioned affair and one of the best links courses in Britain. No trip to South Wales would be complete without tasting the sheer delight of Pennard.

Michael Bennett – Head Professional writes:
Having been the professional at Pennard for over 30 years, I find playing the course a real joy as it tests all your golfing skills. The weather will also influence your round and the course will certainly keep you entertained from your opening tee shot to your final putt.

Pot bunkers, uphill lies, downhill lies, blind tee shots and approaches to greens. There is so much variety in store during this rollercoaster round of golf. If your game is not on song, you can still enjoy the beautiful and scenic views. Here's to good golfing!

Rye (Old)

RYE GOLF CLUB
Camber, Rye, East Sussex, TN31 7QS, England
Telephone: +44 (0) 1797 225241
Website: www.ryegolfclub.co.uk
Architect: Harry Colt, Tom Simpson and Sir Guy Campbell
Visitors: By invitation only

Average Reviewers' Score:

Reviewers' Comments

What an experience! Old fashioned links as it was meant to be... I finally managed to play Rye after 12 years of trying and I have to say I was disappointed... Rye was one of the most interesting courses I have played in England... I always look forward to playing it, mainly because they have some of the finest links greens in the country but the course itself is a bit hit and miss... Amazing... A proper links course, if you ever manage to get a tee time that is... Not as difficult to get on as they say, just contact them on their website in advance... Some of the fastest greens in the country... Super slick greens and in great condition throughout... Some of the par 4s are as tough as anywhere... 3, 4, and 13 were memorable... Traditional through and through, but somewhat spoilt on the turn with holes 10 and 11, which are more parkland-like and 17, which is a nothing hole... Nothing special at all... Courses don't have to be over 7,000 yards to be hard... A wonderful experience and well worth a visit... I would definitely play here again.

So, we've arrived at Rye, but will we get a game? Well, Rye Golf Club is so very private that it is exceedingly difficult to secure a tee time. But wait a minute... the club has recently launched a new website and many say it is now easier to get a game.

Rye was founded in 1894 and a young 25-year-old Harry Colt laid out the course – surely one of the most impressive debut designs in history. Colt later became Rye's secretary. Today's layout bears the hallmark of Tom Simpson and Sir Guy Campbell, though the Second World War almost obliterated the links and a flying bomb almost destroyed the clubhouse. But, thanks to the faithful few, Rye rose up like a phoenix.

With a measly par of 68, and a course that measures over 6,300 yards, Rye has to be one of the toughest courses in Britain. The one and only par five hits us straight away and it comes too early in the round to take too much advantage. The five short holes are outstanding but brutal, with alarmingly elusive elevated greens. The remaining twelve par fours are there for the taking – well, three of them at least. Nine others, yes nine, measure more than 400 yards in length.

Donald Steel writes:
My golfing daydreams revolve most frequently around Rye. There is a gentle breeze from the sea, the small boats with their coloured sails glide down past the harbour as the sun highlights the little town on its hill like a scene from fairyland.

No other course can stand comparison with it in terms of character, setting and atmosphere. Rye is Rye and that is the end of it.

WORPLESDON GOLF CLUB
Woking, Surrey, GU22 0RA, England
Telephone: +44 (0) 1483 472277
Website: www.worplesdongc.co.uk
Architect: John Abercromby
Visitors: Weekdays only - contact in advance

Average Reviewers' Score:

Reviewers' Comments

I rate Worplesdon as one of the best, prettiest and most enjoyable courses I have played... Very enjoyable tree-lined heathland course with bags of visual appeal and the X-factor quality of a laid-back, relaxed club... Built over undulating heathland typical of this area, plenty of heather and trees if you stray off line... 1st is one of the most impressive starting holes I have played – a lovely raised tee to the left of the pro shop looks down on a beautiful fairway... Good variety from hole to hole... Par 3s are amongst the best... Par 5s should flatter your golf... Good driving is rewarded... Signature hole is the 10th over a lake... Last three holes are tough and par is hard to achieve on each... Walking off the 18th, though, I felt very pleased with myself... Club maintains the traditions of the game and its beautiful sleepy clubhouse, with its wood panelling and gabled roofs, epitomises the very essence of Surrey heathland golf... Thoroughly recommended.

Andy Taylor

Worplesdon is one of the prettiest and most delightful of Surrey's many heath and heather courses and it's arguably the best of the trinity of "Ws" (West Hill and Woking being the other two); all three courses virtually border each other. It is set amongst glorious heather, chestnut and pine trees. John Abercromby's inaugural design dates back to 1908 and little has changed after almost 100 years.

It's not a long course at just less than 6,500 yards, but it's supremely challenging and driving accuracy is far more important than length. The front nine plays across stunning undulating terrain, so expect some awkward stances. The back nine is sited on relatively even ground. The greens are always in fabulous condition and are lightning fast with some subtle borrows and undulations. The one-shotters are especially strong and the 175-yard 13th is an absolute cracker, surrounded by bunkers and often rated as one of the best par threes in the UK.

It's a real privilege to play this quiet and elegant course where the springy fairways roll gently up and down, flanked by many mature trees. The profusion of heather provides stunning seasonal colour and a real challenge in finding the wayward golf ball. The clubhouse is one of the most pleasant in all the land and very welcoming.

The following passage was published in Henry Cotton's Guide to Golf In The British Isles and was written by Alan Waters who was then the club professional: "Worplesdon is one of the heather and pine type courses found throughout Surrey, not a long course by some standards, but one which demands accuracy. Our greens have only slight borrows and are very true and not too tricky."

Andy Taylor

ENNISCRONE GOLF CLUB
Enniscrone, Co. Sligo, Ireland
Telephone: +353 (0) 353 96 36297
Website: www.enniscronegolf.com
Architect: Eddie Hackett, Donald Steel
Visitors: Book in advance

Average Reviewers' Score:

Reviewers' Comments

Enniscrone is truly my favourite gem in Ireland… One of the highlights of our trip to northwest Ireland… Of the 15 links courses that I've played in Ireland, this one is my favourite… World class at a third of the price of Ballybunion… Sporty layout with some quirky short par fours that never gets boring… Magnificent dunes are ingeniously incorporated into the layout… Could play it for a week… Holes 6-8 are neither in the dunes nor on the estuary but they are still decent holes. Remainder range from very good to sensational… With impenetrable rough and huge changes in elevation this is a test for mid to low handicappers… Tight narrow fairways place a premium on straight driving… This is a course I would seek out to play again… Make sure you put this one on your list… We cancelled our afternoon game elsewhere to play another round at Enniscrone… Stunning… Great Pro too! This is a Top 20 course at least – play it now.

The location is ravishing; Enniscrone is set on a promontory, which juts out into Killala Bay at the mouth of the Moy Estuary. Scurmore, one Ireland's most beautiful beaches, borders the links, while the moody Ox Mountains provide a stormy backdrop to the east and the Nephin Beg Range dominates the westerly skyline.

The course itself complements its surroundings. The fairways pitch and roll between towering shaggy dunes. Greens are raised on plateaux and protected by deep valleys and ravines, whilst others nestle at the feet of high dunes. There are elevated tee shots and panoramic ocean views. Enniscrone really is a breathtaking golf course with a serious challenge attached.

Stretching out to almost 6,900 yards, it calls for some solid driving. There is nothing unnatural about Enniscrone; it's in tune with its surroundings, where there is this ever-present sense of space and freedom. You must expect a bit of wind, and that will naturally bring another dimension to the challenge. Our recommendation is to play this course before it gets too well known and becomes the Ballybunion of the Western Seaboard.

Donald Steel writes:
Enniscrone's mighty links boast holes lapped by the Atlantic Ocean, the result of one of the most dramatic transformations any course has undergone. To an Irish course that already has its admirers, has been added a series of glorious holes threading a path through mountainous dunes. With such a true flavour of links, it will have few peers.

ABERDOVEY GOLF CLUB
Tywyn Road, Aberdovey, Gwynedd, LL35 0RT, Wales
Telephone: +44 (0) 1654 767493
Website: www.aberdoveygolf.co.uk
Architect: Herbert Fowler, Harry Colt and James Braid
Visitors: Welcome - contact in advance

Average Reviewers' Score:

Reviewers' Comments
Wonderful natural links course... A real treat... Lives in the shadow of Harlech but it needn't, it's a great course in its own right... Not as tough as some of the other links courses in North Wales... It's a bit of a trek to get here but it's worth every ounce of effort... You are assured of a fair test of golf here... Holes are varied and therefore interesting... Opens up with a gentle par four... Par three 3rd is a real tester, a semi blind tee-shot into a heavily guarded green – make sure your game is tuned in from the off... The other par threes all offer up a different examination of your golf game... 12th is a stunning par three and a par here will feel like an eagle... Short par four 16th is a true classic, skirting the railway line. It's a brave golfer who attempts to hit this sloping green from the tee... Greens are reputably the best in Wales... Must be the friendliest club in the world and they've got one of the best links courses too... Recently refurbished clubhouse is a fitting end to this gem in the Dovey estuary... It has to be played.

Aberdovey Golf Club

Aberdovey Golf Club is set enchantingly within the Snowdonia National Park at the mouth of the Dovey Estuary, and the links are wedged between the Cambrian Mountain range and the shore.

A great deal has changed since 1886 when the legendary founder, Colonel Ruck, sank nine flowerpots in the marsh. The hands of many great architects have since touched Aberdovey: Herbert Fowler, Harry Colt and James Braid. It is not surprising that it is such a revered links.

Despite its old age, Aberdovey is no shorty, measuring over 6,500 yards from the back tees. It will test, and has tested, the very best golfers, playing host to a number of amateur championships over the years and it was here as a youngster, that Ian Woosnam developed his craft. It isn't the hardest links course in the British Isles by any stretch of the imagination, but when the wind blows, it can throw the ball off line and into the punishing rough. Only the skilful will score well.

There is so much history at Aberdovey that you cannot help but fall in love with the place. Running alongside this classic out-and-back links is the railway line, reminding us of the days when the trains were full of travelling golfers.

Patric Dickinson writes:
If one dare write about Aberdovey at all, one must begin by letting Bernard Darwin through on the way to the first tee. For this links is 'his', and it is all and more than one would expect from a writer and golfer of such style; for it is both a 'classical' and 'romantic' links.

Woburn (Duke's)

WOBURN GOLF & COUNTRY CLUB
Little Brickhill, Milton Keynes, Bucks, MK17 9LJ, England
Telephone: +44 (0) 1908 370756
Website: www.golf.discoverwoburn.co.uk
Architect: Charles Lawrie
Visitors: Contact in advance – midweek only

Average Reviewers' Score:

Reviewers' Comments

What a joy! Can't really think you could want much more from a course... Although the Duke's is a great course, I think it is the weakest of the three here at Woburn, but having said that, I think it has the best greens. They are huge, tricky to read and, in the summer, as fast as lightning... Lovely layout, great challenge and good condition... Course wasn't in very good condition when I played it... First four holes are absolutely superb, but after that, the rest seem rather samey... There's something a bit ordinary about some of the holes, although all the par threes are good... Some good par 3s... Memorable holes include the 4th and the 13th, the latter has a really tough approach across a ravine to a tight green... Overall an excellent course, but the Duchess would be my first choice any day... I would heartily recommend the Duke's to anyone whether scratch or 18... Give it a try.

Television has turned Woburn into one of the best-known golfing venues in Britain. But in the scheme of things, golf here is still in its infancy. On the other hand, the famous Woburn Abbey has been home to the Bedford family for almost 400 years.

It was Lord Tavistock's brilliant idea to bring golf to Woburn. He commissioned Charles Lawrie of Cotton & Pennink, to design the Duke's. After two years, and much tree-felling, the first course at Woburn opened for play. With fairways flanked by glorious pine, birch and chestnut trees, the Duke's is an intimate golf course. Each hole is played in splendid isolation. It's a serious challenge too, measuring almost 7,000 yards from the back tees and 6,550 from the regular tees. Straight and long driving is the order of the day. This is not a course for the novice golfer – it will beat you up and spit you out.

There are some fantastic holes on the Duke's but the pick of the bunch is the famous par three 3rd. Framed by rhododendrons and gorse, this is a genuinely delightful golf hole. The green is 100 feet below the tee, and the hard green slopes violently from back to front. Measuring only 125 yards, a short iron must be played to the heart of the green, otherwise the ball is likely to scuttle off, pronto.

Alistair Tait writes:
Stand on the first tee of the Duke's Course at Woburn and it's hard to believe this magnificent layout has only been in existence since 1976. It has an old world feel of maturity and tradition, as if it has been around since the early 1900s.

Mature pine trees, silver birch, chestnut and magnificent banks of rhododendron bushes provide a splendid backdrop to a course that is among the best inland tracks in all of Europe. No sooner had the Duke's opened for play than Europe's best golfers were putting it to the test. Three years after opening, the course hosted the 1979 Dunlop Masters. Australian Graham Marsh won the title that year. Two years later Greg Norman made it an antipodean double by adding his own name to the trophy.

WEST SUSSEX GOLF CLUB

Golf Club Lane, Wiggonholt, Pulborough, West Sussex
RH20 2EN, England
Telephone: +44 (0) 1798 872426 **Website:** www.westsussexgolf.co.uk
Architect: Sir Guy Campbell and Major C. K. Hutchinson
Visitors: Contact in advance – Not Tue am or Fri all day

Average Reviewers' Score:

Reviewers' Comments

One of the unsung English gems... Marvellous, traditional and a quintessential English club
with plus-fours, three-hour rounds and foursomes – just how golf used to be played...
Totally beautiful, traditional and a thoroughly enjoyable test of golf... Course is the real
thing and there's nothing better for me anywhere in the world... I thoroughly enjoyed my
round on the pure heathland layout... It's hard to imagine a better course... Its difficulty
definitely belies the Par 68 on the scorecard... What it lacks in length is more than made
up by strategic placement of heather and bunkers (especially on the doglegs)... Scoring
on this dream course is not easy... I was impressed by the renowned 6th but also the
long par 3 12th... Par 3s are brilliant and the course has a really strong finish... The
gentle opener is the only easy birdie opportunity that comes far too soon for most...
A classic heathland course... It won't test the tour pros but it will put a smile on every
handicap golfer's face... Anyone who has not played here is missing a complete treat.

We make no apology for declaring that West Sussex Golf Club is one of our favourite inland courses. It is sheer delight to play golf on this charming sandy outcrop of heathland. The course occupies a priceless, stunning, undulating site on the northern edge of the South Downs.

In the scheme of things, West Sussex is a relative youngster, dating back to 1930. Sir Guy Campbell and Major C K Hutchinson designed the course and these two architects created one of the most natural and aesthetically pleasing golf courses in England.

On the surface of it, West Sussex is a short course, measuring 6,200 yards from the back tees, but you will do very well to play to your handicap and it's unlikely that you will get the impression that the course is short. Clearly, this isn't a championship course but it will provide a challenging and thought-provoking round for the very best golfers whilst remaining enjoyable for the higher handicapper.

The holes wind their way through enchanting woodland, with oak, silver birch and pine providing a pretty backdrop and the heather and the cunning bunkering providing the definition. The colours, especially in autumn, are breathtaking. Each hole demands thought and holds attention, there is a great deal of variation to the holes and many are memorable.

There isn't a signature hole as such, but we especially like the 6th, a 224-yard downhill par three with a pond lurking 40 yards in front of the green; to make matters worse, the whole area of pond is out-of-bounds.

Bernard Darwin writes:
The day on which to see Pulborough, if not to play our best on it, is one when the wind is blowing hard, for the sand is wafted in great puffs, like white clouds across the course, so that we can scarcely believe that the sea is not round the corner.

THE MACHRIE HOTEL & GOLF LINKS
Port Ellen, Isle of Islay, PA42 7AT, Scotland
Telephone: +44 (0) 1496 302310
Website: www.machrie.com
Architect: Willie Campbell, Donald Steel
Visitors: Welcome – no restrictions

Average Reviewers' Score:

Reviewers' Comments

The most fun I have ever had playing golf... The Machrie is mystical, magnificent and mad... There are a lot of blind approach shots and drives... Blind shots galore, imaginative shots being called for... Blind tee shots, blind approach shots, everything but blind putts! Holes 7, 8 & 9, which run alongside Laggan Bay, are tremendous... Too many great holes to mention, but the 7th is probably my favourite... Stay on the line of the marker posts, you won't go far wrong... Enjoyed the solitude, and isolation... Not a long course but well worth a visit... Uncomplicated golf from a bygone era... The lunch at the hotel was excellent... Get on the ferry and stay over on Islay a few days, and when you don't play golf, go to any or all of the seven distilleries

Simon Freeman

The Machrie is a wonderfully nostalgic links course located on the beautiful Hebridean island of Islay, famous for its distilleries and the fabulous rich and "peaty" single malt whisky such as Laphroaig and Bruichladdich.

Willie Campbell laid out this remote links course in 1891 and Donald Steel was brought in to make minor modifications to the layout in the late 1970s. Thankfully, Steel has retained much of the charm and surprise of Campbell's original design, including the numerous blind shots.

The course is laid out across magnificent terrain, dominated by varied and imposing sand dunes. On a clear day, the views across Laggan Bay from the elevated parts of the course are simply breathtaking.

The most surprising aspect of the layout is that the greens are in all sorts of locations – some are raised and some are in sunken punchbowls. The amazing position of greens has virtually negated the need for bunkers and there are very few sand traps here at the Machrie. All this variation makes for an enjoyable, challenging and interesting round of golf.

Simon Freeman – Head Greenkeeper - Machrie

There are many fine links down the West of Scotland and Ireland that make the most of their spectacular surroundings, but for me Machrie is the most serene of all. Summer evenings spent walking and playing between the monolithic dunes while the sun sets over Portnahaven is a magical experience, but the enjoyment of the ambience never exceeds the pleasure of traversing the layout itself.

Blind shots come thick and fast, as the course climbs over and round hills that would long ago have been flattened had the course been situated on the mainland. The firm fescue greens pitch and roll over wonderful natural contours that make for a seamless vista, flanked always by the brutal but beautiful marram grass rough. Few courses I have played have better overall balance, and it is a strength that Machrie builds to a crescendo of difficulty as the course tumbles through the sandhills of the finishing holes.

Hunstanton

HUNSTANTON GOLF CLUB

Average Reviewers' Score:

Golf Course Road, Old Hunstanton, Norfolk, PE36 6JQ, England
Telephone: +44 (0) 1485 532811
Website: www.club-noticeboard.co.uk/hunstanton/
Architect: George Fernie, James Braid, James Sherlock
Visitors: Contact in advance – must be a golf club member

Reviewers' Comments

A classic links up-and-back course, with several intriguing holes and no poor ones...
Total entertainment... We played on a glorious May afternoon with only a 1-club wind,
so some of the course's defences were removed. But there are enough tough bunkers
to concentrate the mind, especially on the enjoyable par 3s... Have played here on
numerous occasions and the greens are consistently fast and true... Greens weren't as
fast as many have suggested, but they ran true and were in good condition... Greens
second to none... Superb undulating fairways... I had not played for 7/8 years and the
course was not as I remember it. The fairways now have water on them and are not like
links fairways at all... Couple of blind shots... Not the most challenging links I have ever
played but still worth every penny... Back at the clubhouse the bar food was excellent
and the members and staff very friendly and welcoming... The course is good honest
fun... Definitely recommended.

Hunstanton is a natural course and a simple out and back affair, interrupted only briefly in the middle of the outward and inward nines by a few short holes that zigzag at right angles across the central dunes. The River Hun and the Wash frame this narrow strip of links land, but you are only offered a few glimpses of the sea from the course itself.

Hunstanton and Royal West Norfolk are near neighbours and both courses are usually rated similarly in the ranking tables. Hunstanton is certainly a connoisseur's golf course, jammed full of memorable quality golf holes and the members are quite rightly proud of the greens, which are tricky to read, fast, hard and true. The rippling fairways are tightly mown and gently undulating.

Two of the world's best lady golfers have played and won here at Hunstanton. In the year before the Great War, Cecil Leitch beat G Ravenscroft 2 and 1 to win the Ladies' British Amateur Championship and in 1921, the great Joyce Wethered beat J Stocker to win the English Ladies' Close Amateur Championship. More recently, in 1972, Hunstanton hosted the Ladies' British Amateur Championship; when Mickey Walker went on to win, beating Claudine Rubin of France.

A feat of incalculable odds also occurred at Hunstanton. In 1974, the amateur Bob Taylor holed in one during a practice round for the Eastern Counties Foursomes. The following day, in the actual competition, he again holed in one. The very next day in the same competition, he once more holed in one. If a hole in one on three consecutive days is not enough, you'll be amazed to hear that it was achieved each time on the same hole, the 16th, a 191-yard par three!

Hunstanton is a tough, full-blown championship golf links; an absolute must-play for serious golfers. Make your score on the outward nine, the back nine is much more difficult, except for the par three 16th, a simple hole in one opportunity.

Belfry (Brabazon)

THE BELFRY
Wishaw, North Warwickshire, B76 9PR, England
Telephone: +44 (0) 1675 470301
Website: www.thebelfry.com
Architect: Peter Alliss and Dave Thomas
Visitors: Welcome – book in advance

Average Reviewers' Score:

Reviewers' Comments
Blown away by the condition and the whole experience… Course is an absolute must-play. It is a bit pricey, but none the less an unforgettable experience… Thought it was really good and got a good deal too… Loads better than I thought. Great feeling when playing the 10th and 18th… Fame for fame's sake… Look past the Ryder Cup excitement and you will find a fairly ordinary course. Ordinary, that is, apart from the feature holes, the 10th and 18th… Some of the other holes are fine too and the course has matured loads since I was last there watching the Ryder Cups… In my view, this is a fantastic course and has far more thrills than just the 10th and 18th alone - for example, the 17th is fantastic… I really enjoyed my game here and I loved everything about it… Course is very strategic and has a very strong run of holes at the end… It's not the prettiest place to be but it is a good well-maintained course with a great history… I enjoyed it… Condition was really good… A superb course and a great facility too.

The Brabazon course at The Belfry doesn't need introducing. After all, it's unique. This course has played host to more Ryder Cups than any other course on the planet - four in total. The excitement comes from playing memorable and familiar holes. And, following Dave Thomas's £2.7m makeover in the late 90s, there is more water on The Brabazon than just about any other inland course in the British Isles – take a few extra balls.

Two outstanding holes have been popularised by television – the 10th and 18th. The former is a unique short par four with water running along the right hand side of the fairway. It is driveable – you've seen Seve do it – so go on, you've got to go for it! The closing hole is also dramatic and dominated by water. It rewards the brave. Cut off as much of the water as you can from the tee, and you will be left with a shorter approach shot, which must carry a lake on its way to a long, narrow, triple-tiered green. This hole has seen more Ryder Cup emotion than any other hole in the world. For this reason alone, to follow in the footsteps of golf's greatest legends, The Brabazon is a must-play course.

Gary Silcock – Head of Golf writes:
So much more than four Ryder Cups, 30 years of golfing giants treading its fairways and two of the most famous holes in golf, every hole of The Brabazon course will offer you an unforgettable challenge.

From the choice of four tee grounds, navigate the winding fairways flanked by myriad specimen deciduous and evergreen trees. Whilst negotiating the skilfully sculptured bunkers and the environmentally exquisite water hazards that tease twelve of the holes, take a moment to feel the presence of the Ryder Cup legends whose footsteps you are about to follow.

Make your own magic by driving the 10th like Seve, or rattling the cup on the 18th's three tiered green looking up at the world-famous ivory building.

ALWOODLEY GOLF CLUB
Wigton Lane, Leeds, Yorkshire, LS17 8SA, England
Telephone: +44 (0) 113 268 1680
Website: www.alwoodley.co.uk
Architect: Alister MacKenzie and Harry Colt
Visitors: Contact secretary in advance

Average Reviewers' Score:

Reviewers' Comments
Alwoodley is absolutely fantastic from start to finish... A top quality course, which is playable all year round... Have played a number of times and walked round for Open Qualifying and the course is a breathtaking heathland experience... Only Ganton can better this course in Yorkshire... Fantastic MacKenzie layout mixing a series of challenging 4s, long and short 3s and super 5s all flanked by heather and gorse... Distances are tough to judge, even with a yardage chart... Cross the road after the short but tricky 2nd and walk onto golfing heaven... It's a tough no-frills heathland/moorland test and it's always a delight to play here... A golfer's golf course that will test the best and you'll need to have your swing intact if you plan to score well... Grand isolation as you play round (the club has a strict limit on members' numbers) and golf of the finest quality... The clubhouse is very unusual... Simply tremendous and I can't wait to return to try and improve on my last feeble score... If I lived in or around Leeds, this is where I'd want to play... Stunning.

Alwoodley is certainly one of the finest and most subtle inland courses in the British Isles, located in a secluded spot. "This the home course of Dr. Mackenzie ought to be good and, personally, I put it very high among inland courses." Wrote Bernard Darwin in his book The Golf Courses of Great Britain.

Founded in 1907, Alwoodley is the cream of a cluster of excellent courses stretching across the moors just north of Leeds. The great Alister Mackenzie (a doctor at the time) joined forces with the already renowned architect, Harry Colt, to fashion Alwoodley. This was Dr Mackenzie's first dabble with golf course design. Clearly inspired, he went on to become a full time golf course architect and later went on to design the great Augusta National, home of the Masters.

The course is a combination of heathland and moorland with rippling fairways and fine, crisp, springy turf. There is plenty of heather and gorse, which provides glorious seasonal colour and punishes the wayward shot. There are few trees, other than the occasional cluster of pines and silver birches on this glorious, windswept heath.

Essentially an out and back course, the front nine is generally regarded as the easier of the two nines (the only two par fives are on the outward nine). The back nine invariably plays into the prevailing winds coming off the Yorkshire Moors.

Make sure that you bring your full compliment of golf clubs. It is likely that this hard but fair course will force you to use every club in the bag. Alwoodley has played host to many important amateur events over the years and it regularly tests the pros when the course is used as a Regional Qualifier for the Open.

Alan C Birch - Alwoodley Golf Club

HANKLEY COMMON GOLF CLUB
Tilford, Farnham, Surrey, GU10 2DD, England
Telephone: +44 (0) 1252 792493
Website: www.hankley.co.uk
Architect: James Braid, Harry Colt
Visitors: Weekdays and pm at weekends

Average Reviewers' Score:

Reviewers' Comments

Simply the best and most enjoyable heathland golf course... This course is just gorgeous; it oozes quality, history and class... A Colt/Braid classic... Design is fantastic... From the minute your starter directs your drive towards a green in the distance, with heather in flower down both sides of the fairways, you know you're playing a great course... A tranquil space that offers every kind of shot the game has to offer... Some holes are tight in places and finding the fairway is a must... Course races off to a difficult start then settles down with some shortish par 4s... It really gets going from the 6th... 7th rated quite rightly as one of the greatest par 3s in GB&I... Holes around the turn are particularly good... Feeling of space whilst surrounded by miles of purple heather makes a visual treat... Most noticeable improvements are off the course, gone is the old stuffiness... Played 36 and would have gone round again... Courses like this are few and far between.

Hankley Common is situated on the North Downs, in a preservation area or to be precise, a 'Site of Special Scientific Interest', home to oak, rowan and the woodlark. The common at Tilford has ferocious heather and a wide-open and windswept appearance. If there was ever a place where seaside links golf meets inland heathery golf, it's here at Hankley Common.

There is an overwhelming feeling of spaciousness on this heathland course, so much so that it seems plausible that a second or third course could be intertwined between the existing 18 holes. To put everything into context, the course occupies 164 acres, but the club actually owns more than 850 acres of perfect heathland. Don't let this feeling of space lull you into a false sense of security – this is not the place to open your shoulders and let rip. Anything slightly off-line will be swallowed up by bunkers, or even worse, by the thick tangled heather.

Eight new back tees are now in play, adding more than 250 extra yards. Hankley Common now measures an impressive 6,702 yards from the tips. This is a really technically testing golf course. Regional Qualifying for the Open has been held at Hankley Common since 1984 and the club has hosted numerous other important amateur and professional events over the years.

So, if you are looking for a memorable, testing and underrated golf course with outstanding greens, look no further than Hankley Common.

Peter Stow – Professional writes:
Hankley Common is an outstanding example of heathland golf. It has a links-like feel and is a true test for golfers of all standards.

It was originally modelled by James Braid and added to by Harry Colt in 1936. The course has retained all its character and the addition of purple tees have given the course additional length that is an undoubtedly a requirement of today's golfer.

Hankley Common Golf Club

BEARWOOD LAKES GOLF CLUB

Bearwood Road, Sindlesham, Nr. Wokingham, Berkshire
RG41 4SJ, England
Telephone: +44 (0) 118 979 7900
Website: www.bearwoodlakes.co.uk
Architect: Martin Hawtree   **Visitors:** Only as member's guest

Average Reviewers' Score:

Reviewers' Comments

Possibly the most beautiful course that I have played... A course which is mature beyond its years... Exquisitely designed course that takes full advantage of the natural landscape and surroundings – an intoxicating blend of heath, forest and lake... Layout is through woodland with stands of pine trees defining many holes... Holes dogleg right and left, there are uphill and downhill holes, and holes where a birdie is a real possibility and others where a par is a great relief... Long straight hitting over water is a requirement on a number of holes... Variety makes this a great course... Course itself is a very thorough test – you will need brains but also you will need brawn... Greens are like glass in the summer... Very well bunkered, with lightning-fast greens... Fine course conditioning is a bonus and the practice facilities and clubhouse are also excellent... One of the best courses anywhere for standard of playing conditions and welcome... Most underrated course in the area... World-class... If you can get on, you won't be disappointed.

Bearwood Lakes Golf Club

The course at Bearwood Lakes Golf Club first opened for play in 1996 and Martin Hawtree designed a thrilling course, which wends its way through the mature trees of the former Bearwood Estate. It looks mature beyond its years and is certainly one of the very best new courses to have been built in the last ten years.

Hawtree has skilfully blended the course into the natural surroundings and the beautiful specimen trees add to the many attractive features. There isn't a single weak hole – each and every one makes you think. The most memorable holes are the six sited around the natural lakes, which cover more than 50 acres. To score well, especially from the back tees, you'll need to bring your 'A' game. The fairways are relatively generous in terms of width but if you stray off this carpeted surface, you'll be in trouble.

Bearwood Lakes is not the most accessible course. You'll need to abduct a member to get a game here. But if you do manage to get on, you will be totally delighted, because this is a course for the connoisseur.

David Newling Ward – Chairman writes:
"The moment that I first saw the Bearwood Estate, I knew that it had the potential to become one of Britain's finest golf courses. I am delighted to say that my vision has now become a reality.

A golf club, no matter how good the greens, fairways and the clubhouse, is not a true club without its members and the ambience they create. We are fortunate to have an enthusiastic and friendly membership who make the most of the many competitions and matches that take place throughout the year. At Bearwood Lakes the enjoyment of our members and their guests is our prime concern. I very much look forward to welcoming you personally to Bearwood Lakes, should you become a member."

Bearwood Lakes Golf Club

Woburn (Marquess)

WOBURN GOLF & COUNTRY CLUB
Little Brickhill, Milton Keynes, Bucks, MK17 9LJ, England
Telephone: +44 (0) 1908 370756
Website: www.golf.discoverwoburn.co.uk
Architect: Ross McMurray, Clive Clark, Peter Alliss and Alex Hay
Visitors: Contact in advance – midweek only

Average Reviewers' Score:

Reviewers' Comments

Woburn's third and newest course is like the more familiar Duke's and Duchess but on steroids... Everything is a little bigger, greens are bigger, fairways wider and course longer... A more open challenge than its neighbours but well bunkered and with no blind drives... Undulating fairways, shaped greens and no repetition... 7th is an excellent big boy's hole but there are few others which are likely to bamboozle you... Finishing four holes will test your long irons... Plenty to challenge the low handicapper... There are two main weaknesses, first is the par 3s, they are fairly nondescript and second is the fact that you can hit driver on most of the par 4s and 5s and get away with it... Great for the golfer who likes to be tested but not battered into submission... Will return happily to play the Marquess again... Make sure you take in the "Woburn Carvery" as this is something to behold... Deserves to be higher in the rankings, it has the potential to be in the Top 10.

The addition of the new Marquess course at Woburn Golf and Country Club puts Woburn in a unique position, standing out on its own as the only venue to have three courses ranked in the Top 100.

The Marquess course straddles the county boundary of Bedfordshire and Buckinghamshire and is set within 200 acres of majestic mature woodland, part of the delightful 3,000-acre Woburn Abbey Estate.

It took a quartet of architects to develop the Marquess: Ross McMurray, Clive Clark, Peter Alliss and Alex Hay, the course opening for play in 1999. The Marquess is different in nature to the Duke's and the Duchess, but perfectly complementary. Fairways are wider and the land more undulating. Trees are more park-like, featuring oak, yew, chestnut, rowan and beech, whereas the other two courses are predominantly carved through pine forests.

It's supremely challenging, measuring well over 7,000 yards from the back tees. In 2001 and 2002, it stole the British Masters from its elder brother, the Duke's. There is no doubt Woburn is a classy place to play golf and now, with three superb golf courses, it is one of the desirable golfing venues in England.

Alistair Tait writes:

Few new courses in recent times have captured the headlines in the way the new Marquess course at Woburn has. Fewer still have been ready to test Europe's top golfers so soon after construction. The Marquess had achieved both feats within just a year of construction.

Europe's elite were sceptical when the Victor Chandler British Masters was switched from the long established and much loved Duke's course to the Marquess for the 2001 tournament. Yet all it took was one practice round for the professionals to agree the Marquess was a fantastic addition to the Woburn Golf & Country Club. Former European number one Colin Montgomerie came off the course after his first practice round and proclaimed: "This is a great course and it has got my name on it. It is perfect for my game."

THE GROVE
Chandler's Cross, Hertfordshire, WD3 4TG, England
Telephone: +44 (0) 1923 294266
Website: www.thegrove.co.uk
Architect: Kyle Phillips
Visitors: Welcome – book in advance

Average Reviewers' Score:

Reviewers' Comments
Stunning new course… Well prepared and in excellent condition… Kyle Phillips has
worked a minor miracle with ordinary land… Conditioning is faultless and the service is
second to none… Fairways were the best I have experienced in the UK and the greens
were lightning fast… Played it a couple of times now and each time becomes more
enjoyable as you work out the do's and definitely don'ts of the course… Overrated,
overpriced, overplayed… I cannot praise this place high enough… Plenty of good-looking
holes with undulating fairways and pot bunkers waiting to snare wayward drives… The
design, like Kingsbarns, is subtle but the greens and bunkering are first rate… One of
the best winter courses around… It's the rising star of UK golf courses… This place is
aimed at the wealthy rather than the normal punter… Fantastic course and so close to
London… You must go at least once… From parking up to going home, this place is pure
golf heaven.

The Grove is one of the newest and most enterprising golf course projects in the British Isles. Designed by Kyle Phillips (the man behind Kingsbarns), the course opened for play in September 2003 to rave reviews and it's already considered by some to be the best course inside the M25. This is not your typical golf club. In fact, it isn't a golf club at all – it's a pay-and-play golf course open to everyone.

Phillips has done a neat job, using the natural contours of the land in an understated way to create a discerning course. Four large teeing areas on each and every hole cater for all golfing standards. Measuring a hefty 7,150 yards from the back tees to a leisurely 5,500 yards from the front tees. The raised undulating greens are simply fantastic, very fast and very true. There are no excuses for three putting here. However, if you miss the green with your approach shot, you can be faced with some very tricky recovery chip shots.
The Grove is certainly a course for the cognoscenti.

Spencer Schaub – Director of Golf writes:
Located on the outskirts of London, The Grove is a jewel of golf course design and five star service. Opened in September 2003, the Kyle Phillips-designed course has already hosted the World Golf Championships American Express Championship, and was described by the best players in the world as the greatest conditioned golf course they play in Europe. The course is generously spread over 200 acres around the impressive Victorian mansion, with the first half being a stern test of long iron approaches and deep bunkers and the back nine demanding finesse as it winds through wooded areas.

One of the finest courses in Europe, The Grove gives all players the chance to tread in Tiger's footsteps and experience quality of playing areas and service, in a fantastically relaxed atmosphere. Distinctly different from any other golfing facilities.

Adare

ADARE MANOR HOTEL & GOLF RESORT

Adare, Co. Limerick, Ireland
Telephone: +353 (0) 61 396566
Website: www.adaremanor.ie
Architect: Robert Trent Jones Snr
Visitors: Contact in advance

Average Reviewers' Score:

Reviewers' Comments

Played off the blue tees, big mistake… Very long and demanding, in good condition and impressive back nine… Adare is an exacting test of golf and certainly one of Trent Jones's better designs… Everything about Trent Jones is bold and whenever I play his courses I'm desperate for some subtlety… Take your bucket and spade and a snorkel, it's a sand and water heaven or hell… It's also a really tough course and playing to handicap is near on impossible unless you're a bandit… As a resort course Adare is excellent, very close to the K Club in all departments: style, condition, quality and service… Not quite what you'd expect for an Irish course but also not a course to be overlooked when in Ireland… If it wasn't for the Irish weather and the beautiful hotel and buildings, then you could easily be on the continent… You can't fault the facilities and the service - second to none… A top-class resort and there's also plenty here to keep the non-golfers happy… Well worth playing.

Adare Manor

Adare Manor Hotel & Golf Resort is set in more than 800 acres of beautiful parkland and formal gardens. The 18th century Adare Manor, located alongside the River Maigue, is an architectural masterpiece of towers and turrets. It was once the ancestral home of the Earls of Dunraven. Now it's an opulent, luxury resort.

The course opened for play in 1995 and was designed Robert Trent Jones Snr. It's a classic Trent Jones design, stretching out a massive 7,138 yards from back tees to a more modest 5,082 yards from the forward tees. The course bears all Trent Jones's hallmarks – cloverleaf bunkers, American-styled mounding, and lots of water. The result is a rather un-Irish, but extremely exciting and challenging. Having said this, there are plenty of natural features and hazards, including the stately trees and the River Maigue, which meanders nonchalantly through the course.

Adare is certainly a dramatic golf course. The drama builds throughout the front nine with some excellent holes, but things really get going at the 11th, a tough 187-yard par three. Bunkers surround the green and the river beckons to catch anything but the perfectly struck tee shot. Still building, the drama reaches a crescendo at the last, a par five, considered by Trent Jones to be the greatest finishing hole in golf.

Undoubtedly, Adare Manor is a dashing, stylish resort, with an excellent championship course attached – one of the best inland tracks in Ireland.

James W. Finegan writes:
Robert Trent Jones was well into his 80s when he undertook to fashion Adare... I am certain that Jones, the pre-eminent figure in golf course architecture during the second half of the 20th century, must be pleased with his work at Adare.

Adare Manor

Moortown

MOORTOWN GOLF CLUB
Harrogate Road, Leeds, LS17 7DB, England
Telephone: +44 (0) 113 268 6521
Website: www.moortown-gc.co.uk
Architect: Dr Alister MacKenzie
Visitors: Contact in advance

Average Reviewers' Score:

Reviewers' Comments

Moortown is a truly excellent day out... Worth playing for just one hole, the 10th, Gibraltar, it's a simply fantastic par three... 10th and 18th holes are exceptional... You are presented with a variety of challenges and all aspects of your game need to be in order if you are to play to your handicap... Low handicappers welcomed to play from the back tees... Varied and interesting layout that provides a testing challenge... Overall presentation was superb... Excellent greens, lots of tradition and very welcoming... Friendly welcome and a great test of golf... It's a great course with plenty of history. Moortown has it all.

Moortown Golf Club is classic moorland golf course with lovely peaty turf that provides the bouncy cushion-effect when walking – a course that is gentle on the feet. The fairways appear wide and inviting – many of the holes are flanked with silver birch, gorse and heather. But don't be fooled, Moortown is no pushover. This golf course is tough and exacting.

It turned out to be a tough test for Walter Hagen, the 1929 Ryder Cup captain and his American team. For it was here, at a cold Moortown, that Great Britain and Ireland, with George Duncan as captain, beat the USA 7-5. This was the first Ryder Cup to be held on home soil.

The holes offer a great deal of variety, both in terms of look and feel and in shot-making requirements and as always with MacKenzie's design, Moortown fits the land like a glove.

Martin Heggie – Advanced PGA Professional writes:

Moortown has always held a richly deserved reputation as one of the country's finest championship golf courses... tough but fair, a blend of perfect moorland turf, immaculate greens, natural hazards of gorse, heather, woodland and streams.

From the opening par five there are many fine holes to enjoy including the new 6th, rated the most difficult, and the famous Gibraltar par three 10th with its sloping plateau green, the club's signature hole. Typical of all great courses, there is a classic finish. With its fairway favouring strategically placed bunkers, the 18th requires two exceptional shots to find the well-guarded green which nestles under the clubhouse windows.

Many famous shots have been played at Moortown's 18th hole. Severiano Ballesteros once managed to fly a nine-iron approach shot clean over the green to the practice putting green! The most historic shot of all was that of Nigel Denham during the English Stroke Play Championship. His approach shot missed the green and entered the clubhouse, from where a window was opened and he was allowed to play his shot back onto the green. This is no longer possible... the clubhouse is now out of bounds.

CHART HILLS GOLF CLUB

Weeks Lane, Biddenden, Kent, TN27 8JX, England
Telephone: +44 (0) 1580 292222 **Website:** www.charthills.co.uk
Architect: Nick Faldo and Steve Smyers
Visitors: Welcome – after 1pm Mon, Wed, Sat, Sun
and before 1pm Fri

Average Reviewers' Score:

Reviewers' Comments

Thank you Mr. Faldo! One of the best new inland courses… Has the feel of a seaside links when the wind blows… Visually and technically intimidating course winding through this beautiful Kent valley… Layout is a real strategist's delight with many shot options presented on every hole and no real benefit to the long hitter except on a couple of holes… Vast amount of bunkers (138 of them) are a key factor but the variety of holes for me is the biggest plus point… Remember your sand wedge, you will go in at least one bunker… Requires the full repertoire of shot making… Numerous challenges, particularly the 'risk and reward' Par 4s and 5s… Only surprise was the Par 3s, which apart from 17 are truly forgettable… Too many great holes to mention but the one for me is 17. Think Florida, think Sawgrass, think island green. Any shot short, left, right or long is wet, simple as that… In every way Chart Hills could be one of the best courses in the country.

Chart Hills is set in the peaceful rural heart of the Garden of England where old oak trees stand guard and where there is sand, lots and lots of sand.

This is Nick Faldo's first European design and the discerning American designer, Steve Smyers, supported him, opening for play in 1993. They have created a big and attractive golf course with acres of water and sand to trip up the very best golfers.

The design is bold and uses the natural contours of the land to good effect. The fairways twist and turn in every conceivable direction, heading towards the huge and frighteningly undulating greens.

The bunkering is daring in the extreme, extravagant and exceptionally varied, ranging from small deep pot bunkers to the huge serpent-like "Anaconda" bunker on the par five 5th that wiggles along for more than 200 yards. Water hazards feature extensively at Chart Hills. These, too, come in all shapes and sizes and are frequently in play, especially on the short par three 17th where the green is an island.

A round of golf at Chart Hills is a memorable experience. The course is always immaculately maintained and the variety of the holes will keep you thoroughly entertained from your first drive to your last putt.

James Cornish – Director of Golf writes:
Chart Hills is set in what was centuries ago the dense 'Andredsweald Forest.' I feel very privileged to be the Director of Golf at my favourite course in the South East.

The famous greens are very large, fast and undulating. In my view therein lies the challenge of Nick Faldo's design. The fairways are often generous but to have a putt from below the hole the golfer must be approaching the green from the correct area of the fairway. Get on the wrong side of the pin and a three putt is likely. The course demands a strong all round game but affords players of all abilities the chance to enjoy their visit.

Aldeburgh

83rd

ALDEBURGH GOLF CLUB

Saxmundham Road, Aldeburgh, Suffolk, IP15 5PE, England
Telephone: +44 (0) 1728 452890
Website: www.aldeburghgolfclub.co.uk
Architect: John Thompson, Willie Fernie, Willie Park Jnr. & J. H. Taylor
Visitors: Contact in advance

Average Reviewers' Score:

Reviewers' Comments

Aldeburgh is a riot of colour in the summer... With a par of 68 and SS of 71, this is one of the most difficult courses in the region... Played here a few seasons ago with a friend who's a 28 handicapper. I loved it, but frankly he just enjoyed the walk. He found too much gorse and nearly killed himself twice when he thinned his ball into the sleeper-faced bunkers! Its sandy soil means that it plays beautifully 52 weeks per year... Some great par fours at Aldeburgh – tough to play to handicap... If you can keep on the straight and narrow, Aldeburgh is there for the taking, but if you are in any way wayward then you are in for a prickly time... Very enjoyable and in excellent condition, deserves to be higher in the rankings... Excellent greens... Two balls only means that rounds are quick (we played a round in three hours)... Would love to go back here in the early summer and once more experience the gorse in flower... I didn't have my camera the last time I played... I won't forget it next time!

Founded in 1884, Aldeburgh is one of the oldest golf courses in Suffolk and is separated from the tidal Alde estuary by an unusual strip of maritime heathland. Although the course itself is ostensibly heathland, its close proximity to the estuary and the North Sea provides a salty whiff of sea air.

It was originally designed by John Thompson and Willie Fernie and modified at the turn of the 20th century by Willie Park Jnr. and J.H.Taylor. Benjamin Britten once lived close to the course, bringing fame to the town through the internationally renowned music festivals at Snape Maltings.

If you play Aldeburgh between May and late June, you will be presented with beautiful narrow fairways weaving their way between bright yellow gorse. You will be hard-pressed to find such an awe-inspiring sight at any golf course. Clearly, you need to be on top of your game. Looking for golf balls in this terrain is a painful business. "I am also very fond of Aldeburgh," wrote Darwin, "though now and again when I am sore and spiky from sitting in gorse bushes, and hot and tired from searching for my ball, I could wish there was just a little less gorse."

Deep, sleeper-faced bunkers protect some of the greens. Combine this with the ever-changing wind and you are presented with an excellent golfing challenge. Or as Darwin said: "I know no course more likely to teach driving accuracy. There is nearly always a wind on that most pleasant heath, and there are very often avenues of gorse, and you simply must keep straight."

Sir Peter Allen writes:
The most conspicuous feature here is the brilliance of the yellow gorse which in its full flowering season almost dazzles the eyes with its golden masses of flowers. The brilliant yellow gorse of East Anglia was said to have been the inspiration of the colour scheme for the engines of the long gone Midland and Great Northern Join Railway.

THE BERKSHIRE GOLF CLUB
Swinley Road, Ascot, Berkshire, SL5 8AY, England
Telephone: +44 (0) 1344 621495
Website: None
Architect: Herbert Fowler
Visitors: By prior arrangement

Average Reviewers' Score:

Reviewers' Comments

Can safely say that the Blue is a truly stunning course… The Blue is every bit as good as the Red with the same excellent tee to green conditioning… It's much more of a conventional layout than the Red with four par3s, three par 5s and the rest fours… Not the easiest opener after lunch and a couple of beers… From the par3 start to the tough par 4 finishing hole, this was a great all-round test with many long carries from the tee… The Blue has a more open feel to it and it's certainly more forgiving than the Red… One of the most endearing features of both courses is the variation of each hole so you are forever on your toes… It's traditional and friendly and they serve one of the best lunches I've ever tasted… The Berkshire is a wonderful club and if I could be a member, I'd jump at the chance as they do everything right.

The Blue course at The Berkshire Golf Club is the Red's more conventional and slightly shorter sister. A more standard four par 3s, three par 5s and eleven par 4s make up the configuration for this delightful par 71 course.

Herbert Fowler was the Berkshire's architect and the Blue course opened for play in 1928. Fowler was actually very good at designing excellent twin golf courses. Not only did Fowler design both courses here at the Berkshire, but he also designed the superb intertwined courses at Walton Heath, the Old and the New.

Both the Berkshire courses have the same natural hazards, although the Blue plays over flatter ground than the Red. Cruelly, the Blue opens up with an exceptionally tough par 3, with the tee directly in front of the clubhouse window. The green sits on a distant plateau. Not the easiest hole on which to start a round of golf – play the Red course in the morning to prepare for it! There are many other notable holes on the Blue course but it's the closing sequence of five holes that makes this a tough but special course. All five are par 4s and three of them are more than 400 yards long.

Paul Anderson – Head Professional writes:

I can't think of a better day's golfing than to play the Red and Blue courses at The Berkshire Golf Club. Just be careful not to eat too much lunch, otherwise you might not be able to appreciate the course in the afternoon!

Both courses are as wonderful as each other, with mature pine trees, heather and excellent greens combining to provide a picturesque yet testing day's golf.

WEST HILL GOLF CLUB
Bagshot Road, Brookwood, Surrey, GU24 0BH, England
Telephone: +44 (0) 1483 474365
Website: www.westhill-golfclub.co.uk
Architect: Cuthbert Butchart
Visitors: Contact secretary in advance

Average Reviewers' Score:

Reviewers' Comments

West Hill is a fantastic course that is unfortunately located in an area with an abundance of great courses so therefore maybe does not get the recognition it deserves... It is comparable to the East at Wentworth but surpasses it when it comes to VFM... While not long in distance, it requires a lot of careful planning off the tee and approaches must be very accurate, as you can ill afford to be above the hole... Not the hardest course in the world, but really nicely designed and very enjoyable... Only two par 5s, which means any birdies must be found on difficult par 4s and dangerous par 3s... Great par 3s (some of the best I have seen and all on one course) and a good mix of par 4s ensure that the course is a pleasure to play... Two of England's finest courses are almost next to each other... If you are ever on the M3 leave at junction 3 and go and play it. You can always tell the wife you were stuck on the M25!

West Hill is the youngest of the trinity of "Ws" located in this most beautiful corner of Surrey (Woking and Worplesdon being the other two). The course is routed in an out and back fashion across undulating sandy ground. The fairways are lined with pine, birch and, of course, tangly heather. Measuring slightly more than 6,350 yards, West Hill is not long by today's standards, but with only two par fives and a lowly par of 69, it represents an enjoyable and testing challenge.

The key to scoring well at West Hill is the successful negotiation of the five short holes and the best of these is undoubtedly the 15th, which measures 212 yards from the back tees. British golf luminary Henry Cotton felt that the 15th was one of the best short holes in Britain and, for a while, Cotton shared the West Hill course record with a 67.

If it's charm that you are looking for, then you need look no further than West Hill. This is a truly delightful golf course.

Guy Shoesmith – Professional writes:

West Hill is truly one of Surrey's oldest gems. It is a heathland course, designed in 1907, lined with towering Scots pines and featuring the brook of Brookwood, which meanders its way through the course, coming into play on six different holes.

In late spring, the course is ablaze with the colour of rhododendrons in full bloom and in late summer, the flowering heather becomes a sea of purple, which requires carrying from every tee.

Strategic play is required from every tee, making the course play considerably longer than its 6,350 yards. The greens have some of the most challenging natural undulations you will ever play and contribute to the wonderful test of golf at West Hill. However, if you are not having your best day, just look around you, breathe deeply and enjoy the wonderful surroundings.

BURNHAM & BERROW GOLF CLUB

St. Christopher's Way, Burnham-on-Sea, Somerset, TA8 2PE, England
Telephone: +44 (0) 1278 785760 **Website:** www.burnhamandberrowgolfclub.co.uk
Architect: Herbert Fowler, Hugh Alison, Harold Hilton
Dr Alister MacKenzie, Harry Colt
Visitors: Handicap certificate required – contact in advance

Average Reviewers' Score:

Reviewers' Comments

Burnham is a fantastic links course which must be played if you are in the area or driving along the M5... Perhaps the most underrated course in England... It has all the elements of classic golf – true greens, a great set of short holes, blind shots and plenty of dunes... The greens when I played were unbelievable – quick, true and tricky and all this in spring... Played in mid Feb in a gale and it was stupidly hard into the 40-50 mph wind. On the 420-yard par 4 8th I hit driver, driver, 5 iron to the green, then four putted as my 20ft downhill putt ran off the green giving me a 60ft return. As I walked onto the 9th tee, I was a broken man! The greens were simply superb as good as the very best greens in summer... Front nine is tougher and better than the back... There are a few great holes in the opening nine with a couple less so at the turn but overall the quality shows through... There are several holes, which any club would love to claim... The holes in the dunes are amazing... Friendly clubhouse... This course made our trip really special.

Burnham & Berrow Golf Club was founded in 1890 and soon after, they hired a youngster called J. H. Taylor. His task was to be the club's first professional and keeper of the greens. One of the great triumvirate, Taylor went on to win the Open Championship five times.

It's a traditional out-and-back links course, framed by sandhills and it's a challenging layout, too, with tumbling fairways laid out in narrow valleys, protected by deep pot-bunkers and thick rough. The greens are fairly small, requiring precision approach shots and once you are on the putting surface, the fun really begins. Burnham's undulating and slick greens are amongst the very best in Britain.

There are many notable and varied holes and a strong collection of par threes. The first six holes are especially good and the back nine is magnificent. Burnham closes with a classic 18th, one of the best finishing holes in golf, a dogleg left over dunes and an intimidating long second shot across another ridge of dunes towards a green protected by deep threatening pot-bunkers.

The club has played host to many important amateur championships over the years and the course is regularly used for Open Championship qualification. It's an absolute must for links purists.

The following passage was published in Henry Cotton's Guide to Golf In The British Isles and was written by Fred Bradbeer who was then the club professional: "This is a testing seaside course as a range of sandhills runs along the right hand side of the back nine, with rough grass on the other sides. Leave the fairways, which are on the narrow side, and you are in trouble. I find it difficult to single out any hole as the toughest, for the wind always seems to be blowing across the course."

WOBURN GOLF & COUNTRY CLUB
Little Brickhill, Milton Keynes, Bucks, MK17 9LJ, England
Telephone: +44 (0) 1908 370756
Website: www.golf.discoverwoburn.co.uk
Architect: Charles Lawrie
Visitors: Contact in advance – midweek only

Average Reviewers' Score:

Reviewers' Comments
Beautiful setting and a very severe test of golf… Shorter than the Duke's, but still retains the beautiful pine surroundings that really are such a great feature here… I defy anyone not to fall in love with this place… I can still remember every hole… It doesn't have the big tricky greens like its brother the Duke's but it more than makes up for it with its charm… Greens are small and well protected… Greens in very good condition and true… If your short game is good, you'll score here… Makes you think that little bit more… Tight narrow fairways the order of the day… Leave your driver in the car; you can get into serious trouble… If you are not straight off the tee here you will be penalised every time… Scoring well on the Duchess is a real test… This course has got be one of the most picturesque in the country… Condition was absolutely immaculate… Highly recommended… You will want to play it again and again and again… Best lunch I have ever had at a golf club… Woburn provides a superb golfing experience.

The Duchess is the shortest and prettiest of the three courses at Woburn Golf Club. Major competitions, accolades and honours are usually heaped on the Dukes, and more recently, the Marquess courses. Nevertheless, the Duchess is delightful in its own right, and a serious challenge.

Charles Lawrie designed the course and it opened for play in 1979. It measures a respectable 6,651 yards from the back tees and it's a fine undulating woodland course, carved through pine trees. It's tighter and less forgiving of the wayward shot than the Duke's so you will require the full repertoire of shots to find the small greens in regulation.

This is definitely a course where you must keep your ball in play. If you manage to do this from the tee, then the rewards can be great. Use your driver sparingly because this is a real thinker's course. The towering pine trees make each hole appear exceptionally tight. However, on occasions, you will need to go for distance.

The Duchess fits into the Woburn family exceptionally well.

Alistair Tait writes:

The Duchess Course is sometimes considered to be the least challenging of the three Woburn courses, the junior sibling lying in the shadow of well respected and much heralded family members. However, like many younger siblings, it's not a charge the Duchess takes lying down. Nor is it one recognised by true aficionados. Anyone who has played the course knows this is a layout that demands as much respect as the adjacent Duke's and Marquess courses.

The Duchess may not measure the same length as the Duke's and Marquess, but it has pride of place in the Woburn set-up. Rather than act as the "third course," it's a layout that fully complements the other two. The Duchess has its own unique features, its own history. And lest anyone be in any doubt as to its place in the Woburn ethos, here's a telling sign: whenever the members fancy a few holes on their own on a quiet summer's evening, usually it's the Duchess they turn to.

Addington

ADDINGTON GOLF CLUB

Shirley Church Road, Addington, Croydon, Surrey, CR0 5AB, England

Telephone: +44 (0) 208 777 1055

Website: www.addingtongolf.com

Architect: J. F. Abercromby

Visitors: Welcome – contact in advance

Average Reviewers' Score:

Reviewers' Comments

It's an absolute dream... With ravines and valleys, it's hard to believe that you are in the middle of town... Difficult to think of a better course inside the M25... A tad short for today's game but very nice to play... Course really gets going from the 7th a tricky short Par 3... 9th is a 90-degree dogleg where you have to cross two ravines via two wooden bridges... 12th is a stunning downhill hole and the 13th might just be the greatest Par 3 in England and certainly Surrey... On the 14th tee you have a fantastic view towards the City and Canary Wharf on a clear day... You feel sheltered from the world once inside the gates... Old, traditional and totally absorbing, this is a real hidden gem... I would happily play here every weekend for the rest of my life - it is that good... It's hard to believe that golfing heaven is in Croydon... Play it and prepare to be blown away.

If you've never visited the Addington Golf Club and Mr Spock beamed you onto the first tee, you would never believe you were a mere ten miles from the centre of London. It's an extraordinary heathland golfing paradise, which has remained virtually unchanged since J. F. Abercromby – the man behind Worplesdon – designed it back in 1914 and many believe it's Abercromby's finest creation. "He had admirable material, the country of sand and heather and birch trees, and with what an artistic eye he used it!" wrote Darwin in his book, Golf Between Two Wars.

In the early days, the Addington boasted two golf courses, the Old and the New. Unfortunately, the New course no longer exists – a housing estate now stands in its place. The current course is an idiosyncratic affair, with rickety trestle bridges spanning glorious heathland dells. Mature pine and birch trees provide a wonderful feeling of intimacy. It really is a delightful place to be, especially in the winter, because the sandy course drains perfectly and remains bone dry underfoot.

The course measures slightly more than 6,300 yards and opens up with a challenging par three. The 5th hole is a long par four with a slight dogleg to the left. An accurate tee shot is required to the right to the left-sloping fairway. A hanging lie is often the order of the day for the second shot, which is uphill to a well-guarded green. Take plenty of club for the approach shot, which is usually longer than it looks.

The following passage was published in Henry Cotton's Guide to Golf In The British Isles and was written by Bill Mitchell who was then the club professional:
"Addington offers the golfer every type of golf shot. The dogleg and semi-dogleg holes are a feature of the course, as are the hanging lies for the second shots, where skilful putting is required on the tricky sloping greens. At the 9th, 10th, 13th and 17th holes, the tee shots are played over ravines, trestle bridges rewarding the accurate golfer."

Murcar th

MURCAR LINKS GOLF CLUB

Bridge of Don, Aberdeen, AB23 8BD, Scotland
Telephone: +44 (0) 1224 704354
Website: www.murcarlinks.com
Architect: Archie Simpson, James Braid and Graeme J Webster
Visitors: Welcome – contact in advance

Average Reviewers' Score:

Reviewers' Comments

Murcar was as near to nirvana as I have been on a golf course, in spite of the blustery weather of the March day… Played at the end of a weeklong tour of links courses in N.E. Scotland. It was not expected to be one of the highlights, but for me it certainly was… Interesting, technical, classic links golf - good greens and great views… Scenery is fabulous… This is a very, very good and enjoyable golf course but probably not quite a classic… Best example of a traditional links golf course in the North East… Yet another of the very good Scottish links… Best holes are through the dunes on the front 9… After a straightforward 1st the course begins to show its class… Some really excellent holes, starting with the 3rd and 4th… Finding fairway off the tee is no easy task… Wayward drives will not merely cost a bogey but regularly double, treble or worse… Underrated course, which probably suffers due to being next door to Royal Aberdeen… Plus the welcome at Murcar is far warmer… A course you should play and will definitely enjoy.

Derek Mortimer

Murcar Links is located on a classic stretch of links land with huge sand dunes, crumpled fairways, whins, burns and heather. There are some magnificent views from the elevated tees across the North Sea and to Aberdeen City in the south. It's a beautifully rugged course with lots of natural of appeal.

The hummocking fairways are sometimes cruelly tight and the ball has a habit of bouncing off the knolls and into vicious rough. Add this to the odd blind shot and you can find yourself leaving quite a few balls behind for the members. Having said this, the experience is stunning and the elevated tees provide that wonderful on-top-of-the-world feeling. The greens are most exquisitely sited on raised tables and amongst the dunes. There is little need for bunker protection around the greens, but to make life even more difficult there are pot bunkers sited there too.

When the wind blows, it's an absolute brute. Whatever the weather, this is a must-play golf course. It's tremendous entertainment all the way round.

Gary J. Forbes - PGA Professional writes:
Those of you who bought the First Edition of the Top 100 Golf Courses of the British Isles book were given the hot tip that Murcar Links was, 'one of the most underrated links courses in Scotland'. Well maybe now it is beginning to get the recognition it deserves.

In early 2006, some alterations and improvements were carried out to the course under the watchful eye of architect Graeme J. Webster, effectively the first since James Braid in the 1930s. The clubhouse was completely refurbished and a practice facility the match of anything in the UK was constructed.

In the summer of 2006, the European Challenge Tour held the inaugural Scottish Challenge at Murcar Links and the Scottish Golf Union has already announced that the 2009 Scottish Open Amateur Championship will be held here in what will be Murcar's centenary year. To quote the First Edition once again, 'this is a Top 50 course not to be missed'.

"A Century in the making and a venue used by the PGA European Tours"

Aberdeen, Scotland
(Airport Code ABZ)

www.murcarlinks.com
Tel/Fax: +44 (0)1224 704354
www.links2links.info

Castlerock (Mussenden)

CASTLEROCK GOLF CLUB
65 Circular Road, Castlerock, Co Londonderry, BT51 4TJ
Northern Ireland
Telephone: +44 (0) 28 7084 8314 **Website:** www.castlerockgc.co.uk
Architect: Ben Sayers and Harry Colt
Visitors: Contact in advance - limited at weekends

Average Reviewers' Score:

Reviewers' Comments

The Mussenden Links is a great links track and deserves to be in the Top 100... A really enjoyable place to play golf... Course is not too tough but is still challenging and not a pushover... Pray for calm because this course is exceptionally difficult on a windy day... It is a par 73 and realistically it could be a par 71 with both the par 5s being reduced to 4. This would not detract from the course... I especially liked the 1st and thought it one of the best opening holes I've played... greens were in incredible condition for October... Greens were very good and made the day... Liked the large halfway house after the 9th hole... View from the 17th tee is spectacular... Welcome in the clubhouse was second to none... Rarely been at a club with such a vibe – you feel that staff are really trying hard to provide a service to the members and guests... Bunkerless short 9-hole Bann course is well worth playing too... I would like to play here again... Castlerock should not be overlooked when playing links golf along the north coast of the Ulster province.

Kevin Murray

Castlerock is a seaside village, located on the Causeway Coast. The course lies at the mouth of the River Bann, where it meets the mighty Atlantic Ocean. On a clear day, the Isle of Islay is visible to the north, and to the west, the rolling hills of Donegal.

Living in the shadow of its famous neighbours, Portstewart and Royal Portrush, Castlerock is every bit as good, and will not disappoint. This is one of the toughest links courses around, with some fantastic holes. Play close to your handicap and you are doing exceptionally well.

The wind is huge factor and when it blows, hold on to your hat. This will no doubt affect scoring. So much so, that in 2001, during the Ireland PGA International, Paul McGinley registered the course record of 64 on a calm day. The previous day, when the wind was up, the eventual winner Des Smyth, was the only player to score better than par.

Ian Blair - PGA Professional writes:

The Mussenden Course at Castlerock is a fine links course. Its main strength is its par 3s which are by no means "Pitch Holes". This is highlighted by the fact that the par 3 4th, Leg O' Mutton is our signature hole. At 200 yards off the championship tee it can be very daunting with out of bounds both left and right, playing to a green that is guarded by four pot bunkers.

After playing five holes away from the clubhouse the course turns at the 6th tee to play back into the prevailing south-westerly breeze and it starts to lengthen its stride with a series of good par 4's, 7th, 8th, 10th & 12th, all measuring around the 400-yard mark. From the 15th tee the course starts to climb to its highest point with the most beautiful view from the 17th tee box. To the east is the River Bann estuary, to the north the Scottish Isles, west to Donegal and south to the rolling hills of Derry, all only visible on a fine day.

From the 17th tee the player is faced with a downhill par 5 with a couple of huge bunkers awaiting both from the tee and the second shot with a narrow entrance to a green that cunningly slopes away from you. The 18th brings you back to the clubhouse with an expectant gallery in the bar taking wagers on one's putting ability.

FAIRMONT ST ANDREWS
St Andrews, Fife, KY16 8PN, Scotland
Telephone: +44 (0) 1334 837000
Website: www.standrewsbay.com
Architect: Gene Sarazen and Sam Torrance
Visitors: Welcome - Contact in advance

Average Reviewers' Score:

Reviewers' Comments

Awesome! Torrance course is well worth playing whilst in the area known as 'Home'...
Truly wonderful experience... Views from the clifftop across the bay are simply stunning...
I'm probably just a cranky curmudgeon but I found this course disappointing... Land is
unlike any true links course... Greens are to die for – proper links standard with speed
to match... Appears to suffer from poor drainage on the fairways... Natural contours
of the land and the dramatic coastal setting have been used really well... Many holes are
designed to offer marvellous risk/reward challenges with bunkers strategically placed to
catch errant shots... Features are typically Scottish, stonewalls, deep bunkers and running
streams, all set in a modern design... Real action takes place over the last twelve holes...
15 is one of those par 3s that makes you tingle standing on the tee... 17 is as picturesque
and nerve jangling as you can get... Strongest last four holes I have played... Hotel,
clubhouse and spa make up a tremendous place to stay...

Designed by the late golfing legend Gene Sarazen and evergreen Scottish senior Sam Torrance, the Torrance course at Fairmont St Andrews is a 7,037-yard layout built on the clifftop overlooking the North Sea. It was constructed with many principles of links golf in mind, offering risk/reward opportunities at many of the holes.

The initial six holes are routed up the hillside around the substantial site of the hotel and spa complex. This introduction offers the golfer a chance to acclimatise to the very fast running greens and take account of the many challenging bunkers that protect the putting surfaces. This is as near to links golf that you will get without the terrain being actually classified as such.

Standing on the 6th tee, a downhill par three hole measuring 220 yards, the full glory of the remaining holes can be seen as the course opens out, displaying emerald green fairways flanked by wispy rough. The background is just as pleasing, with the Tay Estuary in the background and the county of Angus in the distance. There are some fine holes on the back nine, none more so than the 221-yard, par three 15th where the green is protected by a dry stonewall and deep, punishing bunkers. Then there is the signature hole, "Sam's Favourite" at the 448-yard, par four 17th where out-of-bounds runs down the right side of the fairway, parallel to the coastal walkway which cuts into the front of the green.

The sister course to the Torrance is the Devlin, designed by Bruce Devlin. Day tickets were created for places like Fairmont St Andrews where you will be hard pressed to find a more challenging 36 holes at one location.

TREVOSE GOLF & COUNTRY CLUB
Constantine Bay, Padstow, Cornwall, PL28 8JB, England
Telephone: +44 (0) 1841 520208
Website: www.trevose-gc.co.uk
Architect: Harry Colt, Sir Guy Campbell
Visitors: Welcome – contact in advance

Average Reviewers' Score:

Reviewers' Comments

Trevose benefits from a wonderful location on the North Cornwall coast… On arrival you are greeted with the most fantastic panorama of the course and rugged coastline beyond… Is as good as it gets and will soon be the top Cornish links course… Recently lengthened and in immaculate condition with fast, true and undulating greens. It will shortly host more championship events… Excellent test of golf and was in tremendous condition, especially the greens… Start and end of the course certainly are the most interesting… Overall highlight is the range and mix of par 3s which all offer real satisfaction for a shot well played to the heart of the green… Influenced heavily by the strength and direction of the wind, it is a constantly changing challenge that will send you home just wanting to return as soon as you are able… After finishing with a strong par 4, it is very welcoming to then retire to the clubhouse for a meal and enjoy the views across the bay… Everyone should enjoy this course… A golfing heaven.

Trevose is an exhilarating windswept links where little else other than dune grasses survives in the bleakness and also it's a stern test of golf, especially when the wind is up.

The crumpled fairways are generous in width and the rough is kept short to keep up the speed of play and prevent too many lost balls. Some regard Trevose as holiday golf, but the course is technically challenging and will test the very best golfers.

Birdie opportunities are there for the taking on the three short par fives, but make the most of it because many of the par fours are aggressive and supremely challenging. Five of them stretch out over 400 yards. The short holes are also memorable and exciting, especially the 3rd, measuring 166 yards and the 199-yard 11th, with its two-tiered plateau green.

Gary Lenaghan – Professional writes:
Trevose is a most beautiful layout which sits in the mouth of Constantine Bay. On almost every hole you can enjoy the magnificent view out to the Atlantic Ocean and the imposing headland.

The course plays differently every day, dependent on the severity and direction of the always-present wind. The fairways provide generous targets but should they be missed, the rough and bunkers can prove treacherous. Hitting the greens in regulation is never enough to secure par as they slope subtly with some big rises from front to back. Once finished, retire to what must be one of the finest views from any clubhouse.

Castletown

CASTLETOWN GOLF LINKS
Fort Island, Derbyhaven, IM9 1UA, Isle of Man
Telephone: +44 (0) 1624 822220
Website: www.castletowngolflinks.co.uk
Architect: Old Tom Morris, Philip Mackenzie Ross
Visitors: Welcome – contact in advance

Average Reviewers' Score:

Reviewers' Comments

A fantastic links experience and a spectacular setting… Course is virtually surrounded by the sea… Undeniably a true and undiluted test of links golf… The wind is ever-present but the course weaves its way around the peninsula and it is rare that the wind is in your face for more than two consecutive holes… If you like links golf in the raw, this is the place to come… Condition was superb with greens true and fast… 'Tough but fair' is a cliché but at Castletown it is apt… Wild, natural, breathtaking views, tricky greens deep bunkers – Castletown has it all… Keep it on the fairways and you can score very well round here but equally natural hazards such as the beach, the gorse and the ocean come into play… You need to master the bump and run shot to score well… The 5th is a very memorable hole from an elevated tee to a narrow landing area… This is one of my favourite links courses and I never tire of playing it… All in all, a fantastic place to play golf and well worth the trip.

Simon Freeman

Castletown Golf Links is located at the southeastern tip of the Isle of Man, on the rocky Langness Peninsula, better known locally as Fort Island. On a clear day, the distant Cumbrian Mountains can be seen. The peninsula is designated as a Site of Special Scientific Interest, with a number of formally listed ancient monuments, including an Iron Age fort. The triangular headland is bordered on three sides by the Irish Sea and is connected to the mainland by a thin strip of rocks.

Old Tom Morris originally laid out the course back in 1892 and Philip Mackenzie Ross revised it after the Second World War. Little has changed since. Castletown is full of natural hazards – wild rough, rocky beaches, gorse and, of course, the wind. The course is laid out high above sea level and, with no sand dunes, there is no protection from the elements. The upside to this are the unrivalled, panoramic views of the Irish Sea. It's hard to imagine that any other course could possess more coastal frontage than Castletown.

Some draw a parallel between Castletown and Turnberry. Mackenzie Ross is a common denominator, as is the dramatic rocky coastline. Turnberry is perhaps a sterner test, but we think Castletown is more thrilling, dramatic and much better value for money.

Simon Freeman – Course Development Manager writes:
How many links courses can boast holes that run along the shoreline in all four directions? Not many, I'll warrant, but then the site upon which Castletown resides is a special place indeed. A thin causeway the width of the 6th and 10th fairways connects the course and its well-appointed adjacent hotel to the rest of an island steeped in history, with the ancient links rising from this thin strip of beach to give spectacular views to all sides.

The course constantly changes tack – making the utmost use of the seemingly ever-present gale – and winds its way to the very top of the peninsula before plunging down from the 16th tee and into one of the most memorable finishes in the country. This is a truly inspiring place to stay and play.

Castletown Golf Links

WALTON HEATH GOLF CLUB
Deans Lane, Walton on the Hill, Surrey, KT20 7TP, England
Telephone: +44 (0) 1737 812380
Website: www.whgc.co.uk
Architect: Herbert Fowler
Visitors: Contact in advance - weekends limited

Average Reviewers' Score:

Reviewers' Comments

The name is a bit of a misnomer as in truth it's only a handful of years younger than the Old... The surroundings are amazing with heathland everywhere and a beautifully crafted course, intertwined with the Old... The New breaks you in gently and then it gets tough... Simply stunning and great fun... Some superb holes set in amongst stunning card-wrecking heather... Stay straight and scoring isn't too difficult but the heather lines fairways and hides balls amazingly well... Par 4 1st is driveable, as is the 4th and combined with easy par 3 2nd makes it an easy start... Not far behind the Old... Much better than its current ranking... A perfect day is playing both courses, and in this day and age very good value for money! Superb golf club with great food and staff... I reckon that Walton Heath could make the best composite 18 holes of heathland golf on the entire planet... Quintessentially English.

Andy Taylor

The New course at Walton Heath Golf Club was designed by Herbert Fowler and opened for play in 1907 as a nine-hole layout. Fowler extended it to 18 holes in 1913.

Both courses – Old and New – are intertwined and have a very similar look and feel. The Old is tougher, although the New is a demanding course with memorable holes of great variety. Taking the two courses together can only be described as a real treat.

Ken Macpherson – Professional writes:

Together with the Old course, the New has always been chosen by the U.S.G.A. as the 36-hole venue for the U.S. Open Championship Qualifying, which is quite an accolade.

After a gentle start (the first two holes being pleasant, but straightforward), the New course really starts to show its mettle. The heather comes into play and the holes progressively become more challenging. There are six par fours measuring over 400 yards in length; the stroke index 1 is a massive 469 yards from the white tees.

Colourful heather surrounds the fairways and is also to be found on the faces of many of the bunkers. Whereas the Old course has the most testing of starts, the New requires low scoring on the early holes because after the sixth hole there is only one more short hole – the 200-yard tenth – to come.

It would be remiss not to mention James Braid when writing about Walton Heath. Braid loved the Heath and he was the club professional from 1904 to 1950. For much of his life, he lived at Walton on the Hill, close to his beloved golf courses. He proudly called his house Earlsferry after his birthplace in the Kingdom of Fife.

Both courses can be fearsome tests should the wind be blowing and the Championship tees be in use. For the more modest player, forward tees, wide fairways and a fast running course will be a more enjoyable and memorable experience as long as the wind is not blowing!

Stuart Abramson

Royal North Devon

95th

ROYAL NORTH DEVON GOLF CLUB
Golf Links Road, Westward Ho! Devon, EX39 1HD, England
Telephone: +44 (0) 1237 477598
Website: www.royalnorthdevongolfclub.co.uk
Architect: Old Tom Morris and Herbert Fowler
Visitors: Telephone in advance

Average Reviewers' Score:

Reviewers' Comments

Westward Ho! is golf in all its simplicity and beauty – a timewarp to the past. Played today in a gale force 8 wind and loved every second! A wonderful feeling to this course... Links golf at its most natural... Can't imagine how they keep it in such great nick with all those sheep and horses... To start with I didn't get it but towards the middle of the round, I began to appreciate the subtleties... You need to know where you are going and I would have liked a caddy... Fairways are common land, so horses and sheep are commonplace and possible hazards... Fowler's greens complexes are brilliant... I got into all sorts of trouble and lost balls galore... 5th and 6th have to be experienced to understand the wonderful imagination of Fowler... 9th may be one of the great short par fives in existence... Watch out for the sea rushes... Interesting course that is challenging and entertaining... nothing manicured about this one but definitely worth playing... Fabulous venue, lots of history and a joy to play if you like links golf "au natural".

Richard Hughes

Royal North Devon, or should we say Westward Ho! This fabulously nostalgic and monumental links course fits firmly into the "must-play" category. In 1864, Westward Ho! opened for golf and it remains the oldest course in England still playing along its original fairways. It is also the oldest links course outside Scotland and home to the second oldest ladies' golf club in the world, founded in 1868.

"To go to Westward Ho! is not to make a mere visit of pleasure as to an ordinary course;" wrote Darwin in his book, The Golf Courses of the British Isles. "It is, as is the case of a few other great links, a reverent pilgrimage. Was it not here that Mr Horace Hutchinson and J.H. Taylor, besides a host of other fine players, learned the game?"

When you look out of the clubhouse across the course, you might struggle to define the holes. They simply blend into the surroundings. There are no trees or hedges, except if you count the brambles alongside some of the fairways. There are, however, plenty of reeds and rushes waiting to catch the wayward shot. Possibly, the only sound you will hear is that of the wind and if you are lucky, the sound of galloping hooves. Here at Royal North Devon, the sheep and horses have life membership. Don't forget the local rule – if your ball ends up in a hoof mark, you may drop without penalty.

Mike Wilson - Professional
Royal North Devon Golf Club is England's oldest golf course, established in 1864. The course was laid down by god, improved by Old Tom Morris and later retouched in 1908 by Herbert Fowler. It's a true links, with sheep and horses still helping to keep the fairway grass short. The course is a great test of golf, with a real likeness to St Andrews, challenging to all golfers and a traditionalist's dream, with deep sleepered bunkers, hard, fast undulating greens and course design that requires every shot in the bag. The clubhouse is also a museum dedicated to the history of golf, and the club's favourite son, five times Open winner J.H. Taylor.

Richard Hughes

PORTSTEWART GOLF CLUB
Strand Road, Portstewart, Co. Londonderry, BT55 7PG
Northern Ireland
Telephone: +44 (0) 28 7083 2015
Website: www.portstewartgc.co.uk
Architect: Des Giffin **Visitors:** Welcome weekdays and Sat/Sun pm

Average Reviewers' Score:

Reviewers' Comments

Fantastic – the only word to describe the front nine on the Strand course at
Portstewart… Front 9 holes without doubt the most dramatic 9 holes of golf I've played
to date… The first is a great hole and one to get your adrenalin flowing… What a buzz
you get from the opening drive… From the first until you reach the turn you are on
a high and needing the relief of a more sedate back nine to come back down to earth
again… Why can't the course be re-routed so that the present back 9 is played first? If
this was the case most people would leave the course with the feeling that they've played
the best course ever. This is very special terrain with linksland to die for… I liked the
isolation of it all… A large part of the enjoyment is about the feel of the place and the
views afforded of the surrounding land… Liked it better than Portrush… Super condition
for time of year with great greens and tees… It goes straight into my top 10 played…
Altogether a must-do golfing experience… Would recommend it to everyone.

Kevin Murray

Portstewart Golf Club was founded way back in 1894, but the origins of golf being played here date back even further to 1889. The Strand course is a bit of a hybrid, a mix of the old and the new. Major development took place in the late 1980s when the layout was updated and seven new holes were constructed in the virgin sand dune range called "Thistly Hollow". The new Strand course, designed by Des Giffin, opened for play in 1992.

And what an exhilarating golf course this is, set amidst imposing, gigantic sand dunes with panoramic views across the Atlantic mouth of Lough Foyle to the Inishowen peninsula beyond.

The Strand is an incredibly challenging and thoroughly enjoyable golf course, with one of the best opening nine holes in golf. The 1st hole is an absolute stunner, one of golf's most intimidating, a downhill 425-yard par four. There is a plethora of great holes; especially memorable are two of the new par threes, the 3rd and the 6th. The 3rd is a challenging single shotter, measuring 207 yards, whilst the 6th, measuring a mere 140 yards with a plateau green, is also a tough cookie and will stay in the mind for a long time. A golfing trip to Northern Ireland would not be complete without a round on the Strand course.

Alan Hunter – PGA Professional writes:
Portstewart Golf Club's championship Strand Course is one of the definitive Irish links courses. It winds its way through majestic dunes with wonderful views of the sea and Donegal hills to the north and the River Bann to the west. It is a fine test of golf in any of the weather conditions particular to links golf. The first hole, renowned as one of the finest opening holes in golf, leads to narrow fairways, well-placed bunkers and undulating greens.

Kevin Murray

St Andrews (New)

ST ANDREWS LINKS
St Andrews, Fife, KY16 9SF, Scotland
Telephone: +44 (0) 1334 466666
Website: www.standrews.org.uk
Architect: Old Tom Morris, B. Hall Blyth
Visitors: Book at least one month in advance

Average Reviewers' Score:

Reviewers' Comments

Let's get the record straight, this is a very good golf course... It is, in my humble opinion, nothing like its illustrious next-door neighbour... The New is far fairer with wide fairways and flatter greens... Played the New several times, and none of the holes seem particularly memorable... When you reach the estuary, the holes become interesting... Nearly every hole requires good shot making... Ever-present gorse bushes give the course a great deal of definition... Poor shots will be dealt with more harshly than on the Old... This is links golf at near the highest level and a natural, well thought-out design by Old Tom... Last hole finishes with a grandstand-style finish with one of the clubhouse balconies overlooking the green... History, atmosphere, welcome and the paperwork make it all a worthwhile experience... Clubhouse facilities are first class and becoming of a world-sporting venue... Do not miss this course if you are in St. Andrews. Playing the Old and the New will be a links golf experience you will enjoy and won't forget.

Kevin Murray

The New course was designed by Old Tom Morris and B. Hall Blyth and opened for play in 1895. This makes it one of the oldest "new" courses in the world!

Situated adjacent to the Old course, the New is often referred to as the local's favourite because it is tighter and more defined than the Old. It possesses some similarities to the Old, shared fairways, a double green at the 3rd and 15th and the traditional out and back layout. Swathes of dense gorse provide brilliance of seasonal colour.

The fairways are undulating, but they don't have the same slopes and curves as the Old. Consequently, there are fewer hanging lies. There are some great holes on the New, especially in the dunes around the turn for home.

We think that if the New Course could be transported to virtually any other coastal stretch of the British Isles, away from the shadow of its auld mater, it would surely have a higher reputation. Who knows? If the course had not been in the shadows for so long and perhaps updated to a similar extent as many other links courses, it might well have played host to an Open Championship.

Alan McGregor – St Andrews Links Trust writes:
The New course was opened for play in 1895 and, such is its quality, it has remained almost unaltered since. The sister course to the Old course (you are never out of bounds if you land on the Old from the New, and vice versa), the New was laid out by Old Tom Morris himself and is one of the finest links challenges in the world.

In the great St Andrews tradition, there are shared fairways and one double green, but players of the New course will find this gem has a dazzling array of facets that are all its own.

Kevin Murray

LINDRICK GOLF CLUB
Lindrick Common, Worksop, Notts, S81 8BH, England
Telephone: +44 (0) 1909 475282
Website: www.lindrickgolfclub.co.uk
Architect: Tom Dunn, Fred Hawtree
Visitors: Contact in advance – not Tue and weekends

Average Reviewers' Score:

Reviewers' Comments
Just about the friendliest welcome in golf… A great course with excellent crisp turf.
Testing for the very best players… The course has moorland cum heathland feel…
Categorising Lindrick is quite difficult…it's not really heathland, nor is it moorland, but
whatever it is, it makes for great golf… Course is a picture in the spring when the gorse
is in bloom… Course in superb condition with well-drained fairways and firm, fast greens,
even in winter… The best holes are across the busy road (mind how you go when you
cross over)… Has some of the truest and fastest greens I've ever played on in England…
Bring your best putting game… The bunkering is a delight and the course provides a
true challenge for the handicap golfer… With so much history and tradition, Lindrick is a
must-play course… It's a genuinely delightful place to play golf… Bring your jacket and tie
along if you want to drink or eat in the main bar… Fantastic historic clubhouse with the
Ryder Cup room for those not wanting to wear a jacket and tie… Try it alongside Notts.

Lindrick Golf Club is remembered passionately because it was here in 1957 that Great Britain and Ireland beat the USA to win the Ryder Cup. Victory had been a long time coming; the last time GB&I had defeated the dominant Americans was way back in 1933 at Southport & Ainsdale. After the 1957 Lindrick triumph, the Ryder Cup remained firmly in the grasp of the USA until 1985 when, at the Belfry, a combined team of GB&I and Europe managed to wrestle the cup from the Americans.

Lindrick is laid out on prime common land and the excellent turf has a mixed heathland and moorland feel. It's a wild but picturesque course with silver birch-lined fairways, heather and gorse. The fairways are generous and immaculately conditioned, the greens are subtly borrowed, lightning fast and well protected by bunkers. Accuracy, rather than length, is critical at Lindrick. We are stating the obvious here, but it is much more desirable to play from manicured fairways than dense rough.

There are a number of strong holes and the 4th, a short par five of 478 yards, is certainly fun and memorable, with a downhill drive and a blind approach to a hidden green, nestling in a hollow. The 18th is a 210-yard par three. It's unusual to end with a par three and cruel to have such an exacting final tee shot, especially if the match is finely poised.

The following passage was published in Henry Cotton's Guide to Golf In The British Isles and was written by John Jacobs who was then the club professional: "When I came to Lindrick in 1924, as an assistant professional, the course was open common land, but since then oaks and silver birches have been planted... The 472-yard 4th hole causes the most trouble as you are playing a blind second into the green. Bernard Darwin, our great golf scribe, said this hole was the worst on the course, but he added that it must never, on any account, be altered."

Royal Ashdown Forest (Old)

ROYAL ASHDOWN FOREST GOLF CLUB
Chapel Lane, Forest Row, East Sussex, RH18 5LR, England
Telephone: +44 (0) 1342 822018
Website: www.royalashdown.co.uk
Architect: Archdeacon Scott
Visitors: Restrictions Tue and weekends – contact in advance

Average Reviewers' Score:

Reviewers' Comments

A terrific course in a beautiful setting… What a lovely course… It's not a course for novice golfers… some of the carries are fairly daunting and there is thick, ball-eating heather waiting if you miss the fairways… Not too long but plenty of variety and some carries to concentrate the mind off the tee… There have been some subtle changes made to the course in recent years… New tees have been constructed on the 7th and 13th… The 5th has been reshaped… Some trees and furze bushes have recently been removed, which has vastly improved the course… The course is playing better than ever… Greens were excellent, smooth and bobble-free but never easy… Always in good condition, although it can get quite hard and bouncy in summer… If you want a fun, not overly long, tricky, challenging golf course then this is for you… Will definitely want to return, not least because of the friendly attitude of all the staff, from the Secretary's Office to the Pro Shop and bar staff… A fantastic round of golf.

Kevin Murray

Winnie the Pooh and Christopher Robin had many adventures here in the dark and mysterious Ashdown Forest. Winnie invented "Poohsticks" here, a game we reckon is even more popular than golf! Oh, and by the way, watch out for bouncing Tigger.

The Ashdown Forest is protected by Acts of Parliament – no alterations are allowed to the terrain without the conservators' approval. It is doubtful that the course would have remained so naturally beautiful without having these restrictions in place.

The 6th, the "Island Hole", is one of the best short holes anywhere. It's only 125 yards long from the medal tees, but it's fraught with danger, surrounded by a deep stream and a gully. If you hit the green, well done, but two-putting is not easy. There is a ridge running right across the middle of the green.

Martyn Landsborough – Head Professional writes:
If you go down to the woods today at Royal Ashdown Forest Golf Club the only surprise you will get is that after over 100 years of play very little has changed. The fact that the course has no sand bunkers at first seems to detract from the difficulty of the course but nothing could be further from the truth. The sloping fairways, well-protected greens and the heather infested rough immediately respect your attention.

The setting is stunning, affording fantastic views from the high parts of the course across the forest and the rolling Sussex countryside. The resident professionals obviously like it here too. In Royal Ashdown Forest's long history there have been only three pros and Martyn Landsborough, the current pro, has served a mere 17 years at the club!

Each hole is different, each memorable, each with its own challenge and each surrounded by the quiet magnificence of Ashdown Forest.

Kevin Murray

SAUNTON GOLF CLUB
Braunton, North Devon, EX33 1LG, England
Telephone: +44 (0) 1271 812436
Website: www.sauntongolf.co.uk
Architect: Frank Pennink
Visitors: Book in advance – handicap certificate required

Average Reviewers' Score:

Reviewers' Comments

One of the friendliest clubs in the southwest and the guys in the pro shop looked after us really well… The perfect place for a full day of golf… Not quite up to the standard of the truly fantastic East course… A few of us enjoyed the West course more than the East… The wild and rugged sand dune setting make this an inspirational place to play golf… Fast greens, some blind shots, and is a great little links course in its own right… From an interest perspective, I think the West has an edge over the East… "Pulpit", the par 3 16th is a cracking hole but honestly there are no weak holes on the course… It's not of championship length, but it has everything going for it and it's an exacting test of golf… You need to be on top of your course management and have your wits about you, especially off the tee… Plenty of nuances here… With two courses of this quality, Saunton should be at the top of any serious golfer's must-play list… It's fabulous and a must for links lovers… The West is definitely the real deal… It's a little cracker!

On the edge of Bideford Bay and the estuary of the River Taw, lie the mountainous Braunton Burrows – one of the largest systems of sand dunes in England. You'll find Saunton Golf Club amongst these dunes, adjacent to the beautiful and unspoilt North Devon coast.

The West is the second course at Saunton and it's shorter than its older sister – the East – but, nonetheless, the West represents a fine test, measuring 6,403 yards from the medal tees. Host to a number of County Championships and the EGU Seniors Championship, it challenges the very best golfers and is a worthy understudy to the East.

Both courses at Saunton have par set at 71, but the configuration of holes on the West's inward nine is unusual. Three back-to-back par fours in the middle and three par threes and three par fives interspersed at the beginning, and then again, at the end. A number of narrow streams come into play and many of the holes feature doglegs. Apart from the opening hole, which plays directly through towering dunes, the rest of the course plays over pleasant undulating links land, where the dunes are far less imposing.

Albert MacKenzie - Club Professional writes:

Saunton West is the perfect sidekick for its wonderful partner, the East. Club selection from the tee is paramount as positioning the ball is the key to successfully negotiating your way round the West.

The two opening holes, dogleg in nature, set the tone for what is to follow and too much club from the tee can prove disastrous. The West is graced with five par 3s, all different in distance and direction, and a variety of clubs will be required to find the targets. The "loop" on the back nine, comprising the 12th, 13th and 14th, is arguably the best stretch of golfing terrain offered by Saunton, and it will prove to be as testing in nature as it is pleasing to the eye.

Having co-hosted many national Championships alongside the East, the West is truly a Championship course on its own merits.

Saunton Golf Club

Your Top 200 Courses

In our first book – Top 100 Golf Courses of the British Isles – we printed a Top 100 list based on the average reviewers' score from reviews posted on the Top 100 website up to April 2005. The following list shows the Top 200 courses based on the average reviewers' score from May 2005 – Dec 2006. We can't promise it's the most definitive list in existence but it's based on the views of thousands of passionate golfers who have taken the time to write course reviews and rate each course individually. We'll take this Top 200 list and blend it into our ranking database. This book would not be complete without showing the Top 100 (or in this case 200) list according to our visitors' reviews posted on the Top 100 website (www.top100golfcourses. co.uk). We actively encourage people to post reviews and to rate the courses. We think this Top 200 list is absolutely fascinating and perhaps in the next edition of this book, we'll print our entire list (circa 500) of Britain & Ireland's greatest golf courses.

Pos	Course	Move			
1	Royal County Down	Up 1	43	Hindhead	New
2	Turnberry (Ailsa)	Up 5	44	Ballyliffin (Glashedy)	Up 26
3	Carne	Up 19	45	Doonbeg	Down 20
4	Kingsbarns	No Move	46	Saunton (East)	Down 13
5	Royal Dornoch (Championship)	Down 4	47	Belfry (Brabazon)	New
6	St Andrews (Old)	Up 10	48	Gleneagles (King's)	Up 28
7	Muirfield	Up 20	49	Royal Portrush (Valley)	New
8	Woodhall Spa (Hotchkin)	Up 2	50	Crail (Balcomie)	New
9	Lahinch (Old)	Down 6	51	Royal Lytham & St Annes	Up 35
10	Ganton	Up 8	52	Ring of Kerry	New
11	Royal Aberdeen	Down 6	53	Brora	New
12	Royal Birkdale	No move	54	Woburn (Duchess)	Down 28
13	Carnoustie (Championship)	Down 4	55	Worplesdon	Up 16
14	Royal Portrush (Dunluce)	Up 1	56	Gullane (No.1)	New
15	Hankley Common	Up 83	57	Machynys Peninsula	New
16	Rosapenna (Sandy Hills)	Up 26	58	Sunningdale (Old)	Down 25
17	St George's Hill	Down 4	59	Notts	Down 23
18	Enniscrone	Up 29	60	Swinley Forest	Up 4
19	Waterville	Up 38	61	Grove	New
20	Prestwick	Up 18	62	Moor Allerton	New
21	Ballybunion (Old)	Down 13	63	Royal Ashdown Forest (Old)	Up 29
22	Hillside	Up 36	64	Fota Island	New
23	Silloth-on-Solway	Up 33	65	St Mellion (Nicklaus)	New
24	Old Head	Up 5	66	Cruit Island	New
25	Machrihanish	Up 14	67	East Sussex National (West)	New
26	Royal West Norfolk	Up 19	68	Moortown	New
27	Cruden Bay	Up 1	69	Bamburgh Castle	New
28	Royal Porthcawl	Up 49	70	Headfort (New)	New
29	Addington	New	71	Sherwood Forest	New
30	Bearwood Lakes	New	72	Ferndown (Old)	New
31	Pennard	Down 10	73	Western Gailes	Down 59
32	Tralee	Up 12	74	North Hants	New
33	North Berwick (West)	Up 1	75	County Sligo (Championship)	Up 22
34	St Enodoc (Church)	Up 33	76	Dunbar	New
35	Tandridge	New	77	Wentworth (West)	Down 47
36	Walton Heath (Old)	Up 10	78	Gleneagles (PGA Centenary)	New
37	Murcar	Down 18	79	Royal St George's	Up 2
38	Brocket Hall (Palmerston)	Down 6	80	West Hill	Down 29
39	Nairn	Up 10	81	Chart Hills	Down 28
40	Loch Lomond	Down 34	82	Connemara	New
41	European Club	Down 6	83	Castlerock	Down 63
42	Palmerstown House (PGA National)	New	84	Dundonald	New
			85	Copt Heath	New

86	Dromoland Castle	New	144	Glasgow Gailes	New
87	Elie	New	145	Lundin	New
88	Royal Liverpool	New	146	Monifieth (Medal)	New
89	Ballybunion (Cashen)	New	147	Southerndown	New
90	Gullane (No.3)	New	148	Southerness	New
91	Ballyliffin (Old)	Down 11	149	Troon Darley	New
92	Gleneagles (Queen's)	Down 42	150	Bovey Castle	New
93	Portstewart (Strand)	Down 31	151	East Sussex National (East)	New
94	Trevose (Championship)	New	152	Turnberry (Kintrye)	New
95	Brocket Hall (Melbourne)	Down 40	153	Manor House	New
96	Portmarnock (Old)	Down 86	154	Shiskine	New
97	Tain	New	155	Blackmoor	New
98	Woburn (Duke's)	Down 24	156	London Club (Heritage)	New
99	Buckinghamshire	Down 47	157	New Zealand	New
100	Glen	New	158	Panmure	New
101	Gullane (No.2)	New	159	Rye (Old)	Down 77
102	Island	New	160	Aberdovey	Down 66
103	Fulford	New	161	Berwick-upon-Tweed	New
104	Oxfordshire	New	162	Coxmoor	New
105	St Andrews Bay (Torrance)	New	163	Ipswich (Main)	Down 63
106	Druids Glen	Down 66	164	Liphook	New
107	Archerfield (Fidra)	New	165	Parkstone	New
108	West Sussex	Down 71	166	Seacroft	New
109	Aldeburgh	New	167	Wentworth (Edinburgh)	New
110	Formby	Down 21	168	Woodbridge	New
111	Isle of Purbeck	New	169	Conwy	New
112	Littlestone	Down 95	170	Broadstone	New
113	Roxburghe	New	171	Collingtree Park	New
114	Mount Juliet	New	172	Killarney (Mahoney's Point)	New
115	Killarney (Killeen)	New	173	London Club (International)	New
116	Castletown	Down 75	174	Mannings Heath (Waterfall)	New
117	Wallasey	New	175	Sheringham	New
118	Forest of Arden (Arden)	New	176	West Lancashire	Down 98
119	Carton House (O'Meara)	New	177	Burhill (Old)	New
120	Delamere Forest	Down 77	178	Donegal	Down 79
121	Nefyn (Old)	Down 97	179	Linden Hall	New
122	Rosapenna (Old)	New	180	St Andrews (New)	Down 107
123	Ross-on-Wye	New	181	Stoke Park	Down 94
124	Spey Valley	New	182	Bowood G&CC	New
125	Berkshire (Red)	New	183	Cavendish	New
126	Sunningdale (New)	Down 61	184	Cork	New
127	Berkshire (Blue)	New	185	Duke's	New
128	Machrie	Down 40	186	Irvine	New
129	Newmachar (Hawkshill)	New	187	Ladybank	New
130	Llanymynech	New	188	Mendip	New
131	Luffenham Heath	New	189	Moor Park (High)	Down 106
132	Walton Heath (New)	New	190	Musselburgh (Old)	New
133	Royal Worlington & Newmarket	New	191	Ranfurly Castle	New
134	Royal Cinque Ports	New	192	Royal North Devon	New
135	Woburn (Marquess)	New	193	Royal St David's	Down 130
136	Downfield	Down 61	194	Seascale	New
137	Royal Troon (Old)	Down 83	195	Batchworth Park	New
138	Ashburnham	New	196	Celtic Manor (Wentwood Hills)	New
139	Hayling	New	197	County Louth	Down 104
140	Ardglass	New	198	Hesketh	New
141	Prince's	New	199	Powfoot	New
142	Boat of Garten	New	200	Alwoodley	Down 131
143	Carton House (Montgomerie)	New			

Century Up for Mr Top 100

Name: Shaun Rhodes
Occupation: Accountant
Home Town: Beaconsfield (originally from Sheffield)
Golf Club: The Lambourne Club
Handicap: 4

"OK – so how many courses in our Top 100 have you played?" We asked Shaun, who plays to a very respectable 4-handicap. "97" was his deliberate and emphatic response. "So which three courses do you still need to play?" we enquired. "Carne, Rosapenna (Sandy Hills) and Castlerock (Mussenden)", Shaun replied.

We pondered for a few moments, realising that Shaun's missing three courses are located relatively close to each other, in the north and west of Ireland. Naturally we simply had to organise a trip to enable Shaun to play his final three courses and we had to be there to see that impressive century notched up. A couple of phone calls and an email or two later, a trip to Ireland was organised and tee times arranged at Carne, Rosapenna, and Castlerock. Accompanying Shaun was his golfing buddy, Niall Baker, who is hot on Shaun's heels in terms of number of courses played – an impressive 94 up to this point.

Every passionate golfer has a course or two at the top of their "must-play" list but for Shaun it wasn't sufficient to play just a handful of the greatest courses, he simply had to play them all. So it was a thrill for us to enable Shaun's century stand and we were there to witness the momentous occasion.

Photo taken next to the statue of Old Tom Morris at Rosapenna Golf Links. From left to right: Frank Casey Jnr (Director of Rosapenna), Andy Newmarch (Top 100), Niall Baker and Shaun Rhodes.

"When did you consciously start thinking about playing the entire Top 100?" we asked as we walked up the Sandy Hills 1st fairway at Rosapenna. "Well", replied Shaun, as he reached for his 4-iron, "I started ticking the Golf World Top 100 probably a year after our first annual tour in 1997. Eight of the boys go away for a week in June playing the top courses in Britain and Ireland." Prior to the 1997 tour, Shaun had played around ten Top 100 courses, but little did he know at that point that it would take him ten years to achieve at a cost of around £30,000. It goes without saying that Shaun has a very understanding wife called Ellen, who enjoys caddying and often accompanies him on his travels.

"On which course did you shoot your best score Shaun?" we asked, after he pitched his approach shot stone dead. He paused as we conceded another hole. "That's a difficult one. Most of the Top 100 games are four ball better ball, but I've got a few memorable scores, particularly the one under gross I carded around County Louth, but Mark (a member of our travelling group) just had to go one better and shot two under!"

At this point we felt certain that our small wager with Shaun and Niall was already lost. But if we carry on asking questions and perhaps hit the odd elusive green or two, maybe we can hang on in there. "Can you recount any Top 100 on course comedy moments?" we asked, in the hope that Shaun's concentration might waver. "Plenty", replied Shaun, "but quite a few are best told after a pint or two of the black stuff!"

As we hand over their winnings in the bar afterwards, we learn that Shaun's handicap has come down by six shots in the last ten years. That seems to suggest that that playing the greatest courses in Britain and Ireland is good for your game and it mentally makes your home course that little bit easier during the monthly medal.

"Did I mention the time when Mark and I were four down with five to play at Ganton?" asked Shaun. "We got it back to all square going down the last and we all hit reasonable drives. You can only see the top of the flag from your approach shot into the 18th and when we got to the green our opponents were both 10-15 feet from the pin. Mark was in the rough on the right and I suspected I'd over-clubbed and started searching in the rough at the back of the green. I couldn't find my ball anywhere, so I gave up the search and walked hopefully to the hole. We've all done this on many occasions and the ball is never in hole, but this time… it was there! As our opponents watched, I pulled the flag and out popped the ball… lovely!"

Our minds are now firmly made up. We decide not to have a wager at Castlerock and simply let Shaun enjoy his final port of call in his 'Top 100 Golf Courses' odyssey.

Castlerock final port of call in 'top 100 courses' odyssey

DAMIAN MULLAN reports

VISITING golfer Shaun Rhodes cut a tired figure at the end of his 18 holes at Castlerock Golf Club on Friday - and it had only partly to do with the driving wind and rain

off the north coast. No, the real reason for Shaun's fatigue was that he had just completed his mission to visit the 'top 100 golf courses' of the British Isles as listed on the website of the same name.

The journey had taken him around 12 months from start to finish and cost something in the region of

£30,000, but it was money well spent according to the English accountant.

"Initially, Golf World magazine listed the top courses and I thought it was a great idea but then around a year ago I bought this book. 'Top 100 Golf Courses of the British Isles," explained Shaun.

"I then started out playing each of the courses and ticking them off as I went. The first course I played was Lindrick where the 1957 Ryder Cup was held and Castlerock is the 100th and final course.

"Castlerock was a good test of golf and I have to say the course is in great condition. I enjoyed the front nine more than the back nine but to be honest there's no bad holes on the course.

That's quite a recommendation from a man who has played everywhere from Loch Lomond in Scotland to the Belfry in England and numerous courses in between.

English golfer Shaun Rhodes is all smiles as he tees off at Castlerock Golf Club to complete his tour of the 'Top 100 Golf Courses' in the British Isles. IMG 4914

Andy Newmarch, a director of the Top 100 Golf Courses, pictured with Shaun Rhodes at Castlerock Golf Club on Friday. IMG _4904

So, having tried and tested the top 100, what are his particular favourites - and which are the clubs to avoid.

"There are so many great courses," he added. "Loch Lomond was a great experience, Royal County Down was also great while the Old Course at St Andrews was memorable - just for the experience and the history of the place.

"As for disappointments, well the K Club in my opinion is just a tricked up course and ridiculously over-priced, while I was also disappointed in Mount Juliet and the Belfry."

Shaun was accompanied on his round by friend Niall Baker and Andy Newmarch, a director of the 'Top 100 Golf Courses' franchise, and all three were impressed by the warmth of the welcome on this side of the Irish Sea.

"We all come from the south-east of England and there's definitely a different attitude over in Ireland. We've had an especially warm welcome and the Irish people love to concentrate on the important things in life," said Andy, who set up the website with his friend Keith Baxter three years ago.

"Things have really taken off, though, and now we can get up to 90,000 hits in a day.

"The site is really popular with golfers and it also benefits the golf courses as people want to go and play them - people like Shaun for example."

With all 100 courses visited, it's back to work for Shaun until the new version of the 'Top 100' list is published. Then, Shaun is likely to do it all again.

Coleraine Chronicle – 11th October 2006

AIDANBRADLEY
Golf Course Photographer

Assignments • Stock • Prints

www.golfcoursephotography.com
001805.962.8466

Also published by Top 100 Golf Courses in this series...

There are more golf courses in England than Ireland, Scotland and Wales put together. The topographical variation of England's golf courses is perhaps totally unique the world over. The Top 100 Golf Courses of England is the only independent, authoritative guide to England's greatest courses. With informed course reviews from thousands of passionate golfers and inside tips from the Professionals and golf course architects, this book gives the best perspective of top golf in England.

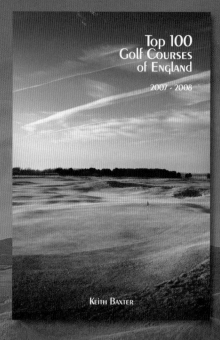

Presented for the first time as a book, the Top 100 Golf Courses of the British Isles comes to life. The British Isles is blessed with many of the world's best golf courses and they are all featured in this edition alongside another 25 great courses, all of which are highly rated by the Top 100 team.

Index